Accounting
In 60 Minutes!

The Ultimate Crash Course to Learning the Basics of Financial Accounting In No Time

By

Jon Woychyshyn, CPA
William Wyatt

Disclaimer

The information provided in this book is designed to provide helpful information on the subjects discussed. The author's books are only meant to provide the reader with the basics knowledge of the topic in question, without any warranties regarding whether the reader will, or will not, be able to incorporate and apply all the information provided. Although the writer will make his best effort share her insights, the topic in question is a complex one, and each person needs a different timeframe to fully incorporate new information. Neither this book, nor any of the author's books constitute a promise that the reader will learn anything within a certain timeframe. The expression "Accounting In 60 Minutes" is a mere orientation given the relationship between the amount of words on the book and the reading speed of an average (and above average) reader. Learning such a complex topic could potentially take much more considering each reader's circumstances.

Table of Contents

Dedicated to those who love going beyond their own frontiers.

Keep on pushing,

Jon Woychyshyn, CPA

William Wyatt

INTRODUCTION
Why You Can't Afford Not to Learn Accounting

If you are reading this book I must assume you are interested in learning the ins and outs of accounting, or perhaps you've stumbled upon it by mistake.

If you are part of the former group you have made the important choice to educate yourself on the principles of accounting, which are key when learning about any business – whether it is your own, or an investment opportunity.

Accounting is said to be the language of business because without a basic knowledge of it you could not possibly understand the financial risks and benefits of a business. Making choices about a business without an understanding of accounting and the financial statements would be similar to randomly placing a bet on a team without any real basis behind the bet. It is unreasonable to expect that such a random bet would consistently produce justified rewards.

Shockingly, many small companies and their entrepreneurs hop into business and are far too busy with growing to consider the accounting aspects of their business. Accounting for them is an inconvenience experienced every year or so when they are required to comply with government tax regulations.

Accounting is a measuring stick for companies to track their progress and allows them to attempt to predict future performance. In the absence of accounting a company flies blindly, completely unaware whether they were winning or losing. What's the point of playing if you don't know if you're winning?

Accounting is required to distinguish the winners from the losers; however, even more importantly it is essential when producing a roadmap for success.

This book will provide you with a basic knowledge of accounting and is ripe with examples to provide context. It is my highest hope it will be useful to you in future business decisions and success.

To your winning,

Jon Woychyshyn, CPA
William Wyatt

Chapter 1
An Introduction to Financial Accounting

Important note

<u>Due to the nature of this book (it contains charts, graphs, and so on), you will
improve your reading experience by setting your device on *LANDSCAPE* mode!</u>

The Role of Financial Accounting

The role of financial accounting continues to evolve as the needs and demands
of stakeholders   (individuals or groups with a vested interest in the entity –
managers, creditors, investors) changes in the business environment. Over the
last two decades scandals involving large well-known corporations, such as
Enron and Arthur Anderson, have shaped the accounting landscape.

Enron Corporation was a large business operating primarily in the United States
that bought and sold energy (natural gas and electricity) in a newly deregulated
domestic market. After enjoying significant success throughout the 1990's the
company came under intense scrutiny in 2001 when the business press began to
question the over-achievement of the company and its stock. Upon further
investigation the company was aggressively recognizing revenue and failing to
record expenses, thereby knowingly overstating the net income year over year
and misleading investors about financial operating results. This was predicated
by the use of internal accounting policies within Enron.

From 2001 to 2002 the stock value of the company plummeted from $80 per
share to pennies per share. The auditors responsible for the annual audit of the
corporation, Arthur Anderson, provided an opinion that Enron's financial
statements were materially correct, despite knowing there were numerous
errors and an overstatement in earnings.

Arthur Anderson attempted to cover up their knowledge of the errors by
deleting emails and shredding documents, however, they were found guilty of
obstruction of justice. The ruling was eventually overturned but the reputation
of the accounting firm had been damaged beyond repair and the accounting
company was put out of business.

The Enron scandal increased the demand for transparency in financial reporting
to arm stakeholders with the information required to make investment
decisions. The Sarbanes-Oxley Act 2002 (SOX) act was created as fallout from this

scandal. SOX is a United States federal law that increased penalties for fraudulent activity, required top management to certify the accuracy of financial information and increased the independence of auditors when auditing financial statements.

In the case of Enron, the financial statements were fraudulently presented, which lead investors to believe the company was much more valuable than it was. Once the true value of the company was revealed the company went bankrupt.

Financial Accounting and Performance Measurement

Internal Users

Accounting allows an entity to track their results over a period of time. For this reason accounting is considered the language of business. Accounting is crucial to the success of any entity to determine the business strategy that will maximize profits. Management of the entity will consistently review accounting records to ensure they are in line with expectations, also known as a budget.

External Users

Aside from management relying on accounting for internal purposes, external parties also rely on accounting records to make informed decisions on investment opportunities. This is known as capital allocation and is an important element in any economy.

Financial Accounting and Capital Allocation

Financial accounting in its simplest form gives relevant measurement and information to stakeholders to make informed decisions. This information comes in the form of financial reporting via (1) balance sheet, (2) income statement (3) statement of cash flows and (4) note disclosures.

Capital allocation is the distribution of resources to entities that can make efficient use of them. Entities take these resources and utilize them to increase total value. For example; a bank provides a loan (resources) to a small business (entity) for the purpose of expanding its operations and income (utilization). There is a risk to the bank that the company will be unable to pay back the loan, therefore, the bank charges the small business interest as compensation for this risk. Before lending the money to the small business the bank will typically request to review the financial statements of the company to ensure it is capable of paying back the loan. In order for the bank to make an informed decision the financial statements must be correct and accurate. Every economy relies on efficient capital allocation within the market for resource maximization and the heart of this capital allocation process is financial accounting.

Financial Statements

Communication on the financial performance of an entity is presented in the financial statements. The statements summarize all transactions that occurred in a given period. These statements will be covered in greater detail in later chapters and include:

Balance Sheet & Statement of Equity

The balance sheet is a snap shot of the entity at a specific time with a list of all its assets, liabilities and equity

Income Statement

The income statement shows the revenue and expenses to earn revenue over a period of time

Statement of Cash Flow

The statement of cash flow breaks down the funds spent and received in various operations of the entity over a period of time

Note Disclosures

Note disclosures provide additional information and detail on the above three statements. They are an integral part to the overall financial statement package and should be carefully considered when financially analysing an entity.

Chapter 1 Summary

- Enron is an example of how important it is to have accurate information from financial statements

- Management depends on financial statements to ensure profitability of the company and external users of the financial statements rely on the statements to make informed capital allocation decisions

- The financial statements are composed of a balance sheet, income statement, statement of cash flow and note disclosures

Chapter 2
Financial Accounting Fundamentals (Statements, Cash vs. Accrual, GAAP)

Recording Transactions

The financial statements are made up of many individual transactions that are grouped and categorized for statement presentation. A transaction is recorded via a journal entry. Every journal entry has two sides which must be equal known as debits and credits.

Debits and Credits

Debits and credits are terms that refer to the left sides and the right sides of a general ledger account. The general ledger is the primary document that holds all transactions of an entity. Within this ledger there are multiple subledgers for main transactions streams (payables, receivables and payroll.)

Debits do not necessarily mean increases universally for all accounts. The general ledger figure below shows how debits and credits affect the respective financial statement and their accounts below.

BALANCE SHEET EQUATION		INCOME STATEMENT EQUATION	
Asset Accounts		**Revenue Accounts**	
Debit	Credit	Debit	Credit
+ Increase	- Decrease	- Decrease	+ Increase
	=		**-**
Liability Accounts		**Expense Accounts**	
Debit	Credit	Debit	Credit
- Decrease	+ Increase	+ Increase	- Decrease
	+		**=**
Equity Accounts		**Net Income**	
Debit	Credit	Debit	Credit
- Decrease	+ Increase	- Decrease	+ Increase

Transactions may arise via two types of events:

1) **External Events** occur when the entity interacts with an outside party and a transaction is made. For example, a farm (entity) purchases seeds to plant from an agriculture distributor (outside party) for $1,000. The

farmer will now have raw material inventory and must record a journal entry to reflect this in their accounting records as follows:

Account	Debit	Credit
Seeds – Raw Materials (Asset)	$1,000	
Accounts Payable (Liability)		$1,000
Total	$1,000	$1,000

The above is an example of a journal posting to record the transactions. Notice both the debit and credit are equal and essentially offset each other.

2) **Internal Events** occur when an entity experiences a change in its economic situation. For example, the farmer in the above situation takes the seeds purchased and produces corn. The farmer must now record an entry to remove the raw materials and add the finished goods inventory or corn:

Account	Debit	Credit
Corn – Finished Good (Asset)	$1,000	
Seeds – Raw Materials (Asset)		$1,000
Total	$1,000	$1,000

The Balance Sheet Equation: ASSETS = LIABILITIES + EQUITY

Assets

Assets are items an entity owns that represent current or future economic benefits. Assets are considered "current" if they can be liquidated to cash within one year. "Long term" assets are benefits that will not be converted to cash within the one year time period. Examples of assets include cash, accounts receivable, raw material inventory, finished good inventory and property, plant and equipment.

Liabilities

A liability occurs when an entity has the responsibility to sacrifice economic benefits. Similar to assets they may also be current and long term. Examples of liabilities include invoicing/accounts payable, income taxes payable and bank debt.

Equity

Equity can be considered the net value (sometimes referred to as "Net Assets" of an entity. Rearranging our accounting equation above as follows:

EQUITY = ASSETS – LIABILITIES

The equation now means the value of the company (equity) is equal to the benefits of a company (assets) minus all of the company's responsibility to pay its debts (liabilities).

EXAMPLE: Suppose you owned a home that could be sold on the market for $100,000. You had a mortgage owing on this house of $60,000. The accounting equation for the house would be as follows:

Assets = $100,000 (House value)

Liabilities = $60,000 (Amount owing on the mortgage)

Equity = $40,000 (Net value of the home to you)

Using our balance sheet equation house example the journal entry to the general ledger would be as follows:

Account	Debit	Credit
House (Asset)	$100,000	
Mortgage (Liability)		$60,000
Equity		$40,000
Total	$100,000	$100,000

The Income Statement Equation: REVENUE – EXPENSES = NET INCOME

Revenue

Revenue is the sales of an entity. It is generated by producing goods and services to outside parties for a fee.

An example of a revenue transaction would be a hair dresser receiving cash for performing their services for a stated fee. The service is the hair cut (performance) the fee is the amount (measurement) and the customer pays immediately after (collectability)

Expenses

Expenses are the costs of producing revenue and operating the business for an entity.

In the case of our hairdresser he or she would need to purchase scissors, shampoo and conditioner and other supplies in order to serve his or her clients. All of these supplies cost money and are considered expenses.

Typically expenses are broken down into two main areas on an income statement:

1) **Cost of Goods Sold:** Expenditures used to directly produce goods and services within an entity. Cost of goods sold includes items such as raw materials and direct wages.

2) **General and Administrative:** Expenditures that are not directly input into products but are required for the operation of the entity. Included in general and administrative expenses are insurance, office supplies and administrative staff wages.

Expenses are split into these two areas because it is useful for a user of the income statement to determine the direct expenses (cost of goods sold) required to produce revenue.

Net Income

Once revenue has been recorded expenses are subtract from this amount to calculate net income. Net income is the amount of profits earned over a period of time and becomes equity/value of the entity.

EXAMPLE: A hairdresser charges a customer $150 to have her hair cut and dyed. The income statement equation would be as follows:
Revenue = $150

Expenses = Scissors $40 + Dye $20 + Shampoo $10 = $70 total

Net Income = $80

Using our income statement equation hairdresser example the journal entry to the general ledger for these accounts would be as follows:

Account	Debit	Credit
Scissors (Expense)	$40	
Dye (Expense)	$20	
Shampoo (Expense)	$10	
Sales (Revenue)		$150

Reporting Periods

Entities typically report their financial statements to external users on an annual basis. Often an entity's annual reporting period coincides with the calendar year end – December 31st but corporations are able to choose a yearend that is convenient for reporting purposes. Many businesses will have sub-reporting periods each month and quarter to review their financial situation.

A reporting period will include all transactions that occurred in the time frame. For example, bank statements from a bank will be sent out monthly to customers and will include all the transactions for the month.

The Trial Balance

As you can see from the above examples an entity could have thousands of transactions within the general ledger. To summarize these transactions a trial balance is created in the following format:

XYZ Company			
Trial Balance			
As at December 31, 20XX			
Account	Debit	Credit	Statement
Cash	$1,000		Balance Sheet
Accounts Receivable	$1,500		Balance Sheet
Prepaid Expenses	$500		Balance Sheet
Inventory	$800		Balance Sheet
Property, Plant & Equipment	$4,000		Balance Sheet
Accounts Payable		$900	Balance Sheet
Bank Debt Payable		$3,000	Balance Sheet

Share Capital		$1	Balance Sheet
Retained Earnings		$1,739	Balance Sheet
Sales		$8,000	Income Statement
Cost of Goods Sold	$5,000		Income Statement
Administrative Expenses	$1,200		Income Statement
Income Tax		$360	Income Statement
	$14,000	$14,000	Income Statement

Within each account there will be multiple journal entries for transactions that have taken place. Note how the total debit and credit amounts balance.

The Accounting Cycle

The accounting cycle are the steps involved in accumulating multiple transactions and organizing them in such a way as to present meaningful financial statements for the stakeholders. Typically these functions are carried out by the accounting or finance department, which may be comprised of one to hundreds of people depending on the size of the entity.

1) The accounting cycle begins with the actual event that requires a transaction to be recording the financial records. Throughout a given period an organization has countless events that require transactions. Typically the transactions have supporting documents that are retained to validate the recording of the transactions. For instance, if an organization ordered office supplies they would receive an invoice and packing slip from the vendor showing the supplies shipped and the dollar value. This invoice and packing slip would be filed by the ordering company in their accounting records.

2) Once the transaction event documents have been finalized a member of the accounting department will enter the transaction as a journal entry which categorizes the transaction by allocating it to specific accounts.

3) After a transaction has been entered into the journal entry it is posted general ledger which contains all the transactions of the organization.

4) An unadjusted trial balance is created at the end of the period which shows all the transaction balances of the accounts for the period.

5) The accounting department will record additional adjusting journal entries at the end of the period to reflect the true financial position of

the organization. An example of this would be recording amortization, which is discussed in later chapters.

6) Once the adjusting entries have been posted a new trial balance is generated showing the revised balances for the period.

7) The trial balance accounts are then grouped into financial statement line items for financial statement presentation purposes.

8) Management will review the statements for accuracy before finalizing.

In our above examples you have seen steps 1 through 4 and will touch on the remaining steps in later chapters.

Qualitative Characteristics of Financial Accounting Information

Relevance

In order for accounting information to be useful it must be relevant. Relevance in accounting is the ability of information to affect decision making. Information is relevant if it has predictive value and is received in a timely manner. For example, if a department store was having a sale they might broadcast a commercial with sale information a week before the sale begins. Doing this gives shoppers information about prices (predictive feedback) and provides a week notice to the shopper (timely).

Reliability

Accounting information is useful if it is reliable. To be reliable information must accurately reflect the underlying economic reality. In the case of Enron the statements did not truly reflect the reality of the company.

Comparability and Consistency

Comparability refers to the ability of users to look at financial statements of two different companies in the same industry to compare financial performance. The idea behind comparability is to create a level playing field in accounting standards so winners and losers may be identified.

Consistency is the application of the same accounting standards and methods from period to period. Changing accounting policies each period would create large differences in results and allow for management to alter their results by choosing whichever policies they please. Accounting methods may be changed if warranted, but also must be disclosed by the company in the note disclosures.

Assumptions of Financial Statements

Within financial statements there are assumptions used when preparing the statements.

Monetary Unit

The monetary unit assumption assumes that measurement of values in the financial statements is done using the same unit. For example, an entity in the United States may report their statements in terms of US Dollars and would not have other currencies within the statements.

Economic Entity

The economic entity assumption assumes only one organization is reported in the financial statements. It would be misleading for two entities to combine their statements together as the user would not be able to distinguish the separate position of each entity.

Time Period

The time period assumption assumes an entity is capable of reporting its financial position and operations within specific time intervals and they should disclose the period the financial statements are covering. The shorter the time interval covered the more likely estimates will be utilized by the accountant preparing the statements.

Going Concern

The going concern assumption assumes that the entity will continue to operate indefinitely. Using this assumption allows the use of accounting methods such as prepaying for assets and accruing expenses because the company is expected to utilize those future expenditures. When a company is not a going concern different accounting methodologies should be used.

Generally Accepted Accounting Principles

Standard setters are responsible for creating rules and guidelines for the presentation of financial statements. These rules and guidelines are known as Generally Accepted Accounting Principles (GAAP). Management and business owners must adhere to these rules when creating their financial statements to ensure they are free bias and can be understood by the users of the statements. GAAP differs in each jurisdiction/country, but there are typically certain common principles shared.

Revenue Recognition Principle

In order for an entity to recognize revenue or sales that is consistent with GAAP certain criteria must be met.

1) **Performance:** The entity must have provided a good or services to a customer that is substantially complete. For example, if a contractor was building a house over the span of two months it would not be correct for the contractor to record revenue until he/she was close to completing the house.

2) **Measurement:** The revenue amount must be measureable in currency. In our above contractor example this would be the compensation amount agreed to by the contractor and the house buyer.

3) **Collectability:** In order to recognize revenue the entity must be reasonably assured on collection of the revenue. If our contractor had no plans to ever collect funds from the house buyer he/she should not record revenue for this transaction.

In the case of Enron revenue was being recorded before any performance took place in order to make the company look more profitable than it really was. Enron also never received any of these funds and never expected to, therefore collectability was never assured.

Matching Principle

The matching principle in GAAP accounting states that both revenue and expenses on the income statement should be recognized and recorded in the period in which they take place are earned and incurred, respectively. This principle is an important component of the accrual method of accounting.

In our above example suppose ABC Company received the supplies January 10th, however, did not actually consume the supplies until March 15th. Under the matching principle it would be inappropriate to record the supplies as an office supply expense on January 10th since they have not been consumed. Therefore the entry on January 10th would be:

Date	Account	Debit	Credit
January 10	Prepaid Expenses	$800	
January 10	Accounts Payable		$800
Total		$800	$800

A prepaid expense is an asset account because it represents the future benefit to the entity. When the supplies are actually consumed on March 15th the entry will be:

Date	Account	Debit	Credit
March 15	Office Supply Expense	$800	
March 15	Prepaid Expenses		$800
Total		$800	$800

The purpose of recording these entries at different points in time is to ensure the accounting records of ABC Company accurately reflect the true economic reality at all points in time.

Historical Cost Principle

The historical cost principles required entities to report assets and liabilities at their acquisition cost versus their fair market value. For example, if land was purchased by an entity for $100,000 but could sell the property for $200,000 the historical cost principle would require the entity to value the land at $100,000 on the financial statements. This principle ensures management bias is limited when preparing the financial statements; however, using the historical cost principle also reduces the relevance of the financial statements. In the property example above it may be useful for a user of the statement to know that land has a fair market value of $200,000, but because of the historical cost value this information is not disclosed in the financial statements.

Full Disclosure Principle

The full disclosure principle requires entities to provide information in the financial statements that would affect a user's comprehension of the statements. This principle is fairly subjective as it can be difficult for an entity to determine what information would affect a user's understanding. Information in financial statements extends beyond quantitative values it may also include qualitative characteristics such as accounting methodology and detailed descriptions on assets and liabilities within the financial statements. Often qualitative descriptions are listed in the note disclosures of the financial statements.

Cash Method VS Accrual Method

Cash Method

The cash method is a process of recording transactions based on cash only. The only transaction that ever triggers a journal posting under this method is the exchange of cash. Using this method is extremely simple, however does not always accurately reflect the true economic reality of an entity due to timing differences between cash inflows and outflows.

Accrual Method

The accrual method of accounting records transactions once the economic reality of an entity has changed regardless of whether the change involves cash or not. This method can be more complex and therefore more expensive for entities to implement, however, this presents a much more accurate picture of the entities financial position.

EXAMPLE: On January 10th XYZ Company invoices ABC Company $800 for office supplies which are delivered on the same day. ABC Company later pays the invoice on February 15th in full.

Cash Method

Under the cash method XYZ Company would record the following journal entry to recognize revenue on February 15th:

Date	Account	Debit	Credit
February 15	Cash	$800	
February 15	Sales		$800
Total		$800	$800

Accrual Method

Under the accrual method XYZ would record the follow journal entry to recognize revenue on January 10th:

Date	Account	Debit	Credit
January 10	Accounts Receivable	$800	
January 10	Sales		$800
Total		$800	$800

The transaction to record the payment on February 15th is as follows:

Date	Account	Debit	Credit
February 15	Cash	$800	
February 15	Accounts Receivable		$800
Total		$800	$800

The net effect of these entries is a revenue balance of $800 and cash balance of $800 and accounts receivable will be $nil.

As you can see the accrual method recognizes revenue when the goods exchange hands rather than the cash. In the above example if ABC Company was using the accrual method, they would record an office supply expense on January 10th and the offsetting entry would be to accounts payable:

Date	Account	Debit	Credit
January 10	Office Supply Expense	$800	
January 10	Accounts Payable		$800
Total		$800	$800

Materiality

In GAAP accounting the concept of materiality refers to any quantitative amount or qualitative factors in the financial statements that would affect a stakeholder's decision about an entity.

Quantitative Materiality

Users of financial statements rely on the information to make informed decisions about an entity's financial position. Quantitative materiality is the dollar amount that would affect a user's perception of the entity. For example, when looking at the financial statements of such large corporations, such as General Electric, you will notice they report all figures in thousands of dollars rather than exact amounts ($100,000 is presented as $100 in their statements). This is done for ease of presentation and because a user would be indifferent to whether the sales amount was $99,900 or $100,100 – it would not change their minds about the company because in the grand scheme of things it is a relatively nominal amount.

Materiality for large corporations is typically higher than that of small corporations. The purpose of quantitative materiality is to determine how sensitive users will be to figures in the financial statements.

Qualitative Materiality

While the financial statements are presented primarily in terms of dollar amounts, other qualitative factors may change a user's mind about the entity. Consider an entity that experienced a large amount of employee theft (fraud) for the reporting period of the financial statements. Stakeholders and users of the statements would obviously want to be made aware of this fraud as it may change their mind on whether or not to invest in the company.

Conservatism

The term conservatism in GAAP accounting reflects an attitude that financial statements should always lean towards the side of caution whenever judgement is being used.

When dealing with complex accounting topics management will be required to make estimates or judgements based on their experiences. Management may have biases or incentives to use aggressive accounting estimates. In the case of Enron aggressive accounting was used by management as they received bonuses and compensation directly tied to the performance of the company.

Suppose a company was currently being sued for negligence in the amount of $1,000,000. Based on discussions with lawyers, management feels there is a 50% chance they will be sued and have to pay the claim. The company should expense $500,000 ($1,000,000 x 50%) to $1,000,000 in order to be conservative even though the judgement has not been finalized. Recording this event in the financial statements would certainly be considered material to most potential investors given large dollar amount.

- Financial statements are made up of multiple transactions that are recorded using offsetting debits and credits

- The balance sheet equation: ASSETS = LIABILITIES + EQUITY

- A trial balance summarizes all transactions in their accounts and has equal debits and credits – this is the source information for all the financial statements

- The account cycle is the process in which all transactions are recorded and ultimately presented on the financial statements

- There are assumptions used when preparing financial statements that assume the entity will operate indefinitely (going concern), has one type of currency (monetary unit), report in time frames (time period) and will only report on one entity (economic entity)

- Generally Accepted Accounting Principles (GAAP) are a set of guidelines used to record transactions within the financial statements

- The cash basis of accounting is a method of recording transactions only when cash is exchanged, however, it fails to recognize the true economic reality of entities

- GAAP requires the use of the accrual basis of accounting which matches expenses and revenues in the corresponding period in which they are incurred regardless of cash movement

- Revenue recognition requires performance, measurability and collectability

- Materiality is a concept that measures a user's sensitivity of qualitative and quantitative factors in the financial statements

Chapter 3
The Balance Sheet

The balance sheet is a snapshot of the financial position of an entity at any given time.

A balance sheet lists the name of the entity, the type of statement and the report date of the statement. For example:

XYZ Company (Company)
Balance Sheet (Statement Type)
As at December 31, 20XX (Report Date)

In the previous chapter you learned the balance sheet equation:
ASSETS = LIABILITIES + EQUITY

We will now look at the various components that make up assets, liabilities and equity

Currents Assets (Debit Accounts)

Assets are items an entity is entitled to that represent current or future economic benefits. Assets are typically listed in order of ease of liquidity (conversion to cash) and classified as current and non-current.

Cash and Cash Equivalents

The first line item on most balance sheets is Cash and Cash Equivalents. These are funds held in bank accounts owned by the entity. Within this line item several bank accounts may exist but are grouped for financial statement presentation.

If an entity has foreign currency accounts they are converted to domestic funds for financial statement presentation using the exchange rate on the report date. Any value changes resulting from fluctuating exchange rates are recorded as a gain or loss on the income statement under gain or loss on foreign exchange.

Cash Equivalents include short term investments that are easily convertible to cash. In order for funds to be classified as cash equivalents they must also be low risk.

When an entity generates sales or revenue but does not receive payment the balance owing is classified as accounts receivable.

Typically entities will offer incentives to customers for prompt payment. A common incentive is payment received within 10 days will allow for a 2% discount or the full amount is due in 30 days. An entity has two methods of accounting for these types of discounts; gross and net.

EXAMPLE: XYZ Company provides a 2% discount to customers that pay within 15 days of the invoice date. The remaining balance is due 30 days from the date of the invoice.

On April 5th XYZ Company has sales of $100 to ABC Company.

To record this transaction in XYZ Company using the gross method the initial entry would be:

Date	Account	Debit	Credit
April 5	Accounts Receivable	$100	
April 5	Sales		$100
Total		$100	$100

If the customer paid the invoice on April 9th (within 10 days) and received the discount an additional entry would be required:

Date	Account	Debit	Credit
April 9	Sales Discount	$2	
April 9	Accounts Receivable		$2
Total		$2	$2

If the customer did not pay within 10 days no additional entry would be required.

To record this transaction in XYZ Company using the net method the initial entry would be:

Date	Account	Debit	Credit
April 5	Accounts Receivable	$98	
April 5	Sales		$98
Total		$98	$98

Under the net method the entry assumes immediately that the discount will be taken, however, if the discount was not taken and payment was received April 20th the entry would be:

Date	Account	Debit	Credit
April 20	Cash	$100	
April 20	Discount Forfeited		$2
April 20	Accounts Receivable		$98
Total		$100	$100

Allowance for Bad Debt

Entities typically encounter customers that are unable to pay invoices. To account for these situations entities will record entries to reflect the amount that will not be paid. The balance of the unpaid amounts offset the total amount listed in accounts receivable.

GAAP requires entities to anticipate bad debts when making sales regardless of whether a bad debt has occurred. Making these estimates of bad debt allowances are considered to be conservative. There are three types of methods when analysing an appropriate amount for the allowance:

1) **Percentage of Sales Method:** Using this method management estimates that a certain percentage of sales will be uncollectible in the year:

   Sales x Percentage of Uncollectible Estimate = Allowance for Bad Debts

2) **Percentage of Receivables Method:** Under this method a percentage rate is directly applied to gross accounts receivable to estimate the amount of bad debt expected:
   Total Accounts Receivable x Percentage of Uncollectible Estimate = Allowance for Bad Debts

3) **Management Judgement:** Depending on the size of the entity management may be capable of determining potential uncollectible amounts by reviewing the accounts receivable aged listing report. Ab aged listing This type of method is suitable for smaller organizations that are able to review individual customer accounts in detail to determine the potential risk of bad debts.

Once an allowance has been estimated an entry must be booked to reflect this entry.

EXAMPLE: On December 31, 20XX XYZ Company has $100,000 in annual revenues and $15,000 in gross accounts receivable. XYZ Company uses the percentage of sales method to calculate allowance for doubtful accounts using a rate of 3%.

The entry required to book the allowance for doubtful accounts is as follows:

Date	Account	Debit	Credit
December 31	Bad Debt Expense	$3,000	
December 31	Accounts Receivable		$3,000
Total		$3,000	$3,000

Net accounts receivable on the balance sheet will be listed as $12,000 ($15,000 - $3,000)

Short-Term Investments

Short-term investments are current assets that are expected to be liquidated within a one year period. Types of short-term investments include bonds near the end of maturity, GIC's and stocks that are expected to be sold. In order to be classified as short term the investments should have a readily available market in which they can be sold.

Gains and losses on short-term investments will be covered later on in this chapter under Long-Term Investment.

Prepaid Expense/Asset

Prepaid expenses are a result of the accrual method of accounting. Recall in the previous chapter that the accrual method of accounting attempts to portray the true economic reality of an entity regardless of whether funds have been spent. An entity may pay cash upfront in order to secure the right to future benefits. Setting up a prepaid asset allows the entity to match the use of the future benefit as an expense in the period in which it is actually utilized.

EXAMPLE: XYZ Company purchases $5,000 of building insurance on December 10th, 2013 for coverage starting January 1st, 2014 and ending December 31st, 2014 with cash.

To book the initial transaction XYZ Company will record the following entry:

Date	Account	Debit	Credit
December 10, 2013	Prepaid Expenses	$5,000	
December 10, 2013	Cash		$5,000
Total		$5,000	$5,000

Moving forward XYZ Company will be required to expense this prepaid insurance over the course of the year, typically in monthly increments. Therefore, each month XYZ Company will record the following entry:

Date	Account	Debit	Credit
January 31, 2014	Insurance Expense	$416.67*	
January 31, 2014	Prepaid Expenses		$416.67
Total		$416.67	$416.67

*$5,000 / 12 months = $416.67

The above entry is an increase in expense (debit) and a decrease in assets (credit). The prepaid expense/asset account will continue to be drawn down each month until it reaches a $nil balance on December 31, 2014. The full insurance expense for the year on the income statement will be $5,000.

In the above example an entity has purchased the right for future benefits (insurance coverage). It would be incorrect to expense the whole amount on the income statement when cash exchanges hands on December 10th, 2013 because the coverage relates to the 2014 year. In order to comply with the matching principle the insurance premium is expensed in the actual year it is utilized.

Inventory – Raw Materials

Raw materials are physical goods purchased by entities for the purpose of producing a finished good. Manufacturing businesses often purchase multiple types of raw materials to produce their product to generate revenue.

Raw materials fall into one of two categories:

1) **Direct Materials:** These are items purchased that go directly into the product. For example, wood is needed to produce a wooden table.

2) **Indirect Materials:** These are items that are required for the production of the product but are not physically input into the product. An example

of indirect materials would be light bulbs or oil at a manufacturing plant that are required for maintenance of the facility.

Inventory – Work in Progress & Finished Goods

Once the production process begins in an entity raw materials are classified as work in progress and finally finished goods once the production process is complete. Entities may have both work in progress and finished good listed on their balance sheet as it is relevant to a user of the financial statements to distinguish between products that are finished and ready to be sold and those that still require additional resources to be completed.

The finished goods account contains all the costs that are required to produce the final product of an entity. Once the product is sold to a customer the finished good is taken off the balance sheet and listed as a cost of goods sold. More will be covered on cost of goods sold in a later chapter, for now it is important to grasp the concept of accounting for finished goods.

Finish goods are typically comprised of the following inputs:

1) **Direct Materials:** All physical products that are required to produce a finished product

2) **Direct Labour:** Wages paid to employees that are specifically involved in the creation of the finished product

3) **Variable & Fixed Overhead:** Resources required to produce the finished product but is not directly input into the finished product. Examples of overheads include plant repair and maintenance, equipment/plant supplies (oil and small tools) and plant utilities (hydro and natural gas). Variable overhead are purchases that correlate directly with the level of production, whereas fixed overhead purchases are static regardless of production.

GAAP requires that finished goods be accounted for at the lessor of net book value or fair market value:

1) **Net Book Value:** The cost of all direct and indirect raw materials that are input into the product.

2) **Fair Market Value:** The value the entity is able to sell the product for.

In order to generate net income entities must be able to sell their product for a higher price than it costs to produce. If the cost for an entity to produce their product exceeded the value for which they could sell the product GAAP would require the entity reduce the value of finished goods to the sales amount.

EXAMPLE: XYZ Company is a producer hammers. The hammers are composed of a wooden handle and a steel head, which XYZ purchases through a supplier.

On April 5th, 2014 XYZ purchases $500 worth of indirect materials, 100 wooden handles for $1 each and 100 steel heads for $3 each on credit. The following entry is recorded:

Date	Account	Debit	Credit
April 5, 2014	Raw Materials (Handles)	$100	
April 5, 2014	Raw Materials (Heads)	$300	
April 5, 2014	Raw Materials (Indirect)	$500	
April 5, 2014	Accounts Payable		$900
Total		$900	$900

XYZ Company starts production of 100 hammers on April 10th, 2014 and uses $500 of indirect material throughout the remainder of the month. As at April 30th, 2014 the hammers have not been completed. Therefore, on April 30th, 2014 the following entry is recorded:

Date	Account	Debit	Credit
April 5, 2014	Work in Progress	$900	
April 5, 2014	Raw Materials (Indirect)		$500
April 5, 2014	Raw Materials (Handles)		$100
April 5, 2014	Raw Materials (Heads)		$300
Total		$900	$900

The above entry clears out the raw materials account and places it under work in progress on the balance sheet of XYZ.

On May 31st the 100 hammers are completed and ready for sale. The entry to reclassify the goods as finished is:

Date	Account	Debit	Credit

May 31, 2014	Finished Goods	$900	
May 13, 2014	Work in Progress		$900
Total		$900	$900

Therefore, each hammer cost XYZ Company $9 each to produce ($900 / 100 hammers).

On June 8th, 2014 XYZ sells 50 if the hammers for $20 each in cash. The entry to record the reduction in inventory is:

Date	Account	Debit	Credit
May 31, 2014	Cost of Goods Sold	$450*	
May 31, 2014	Finished Goods		$450
Total		$450	$450

*$9 x 50 hammers = $450

Inventory Methods

Entities typically conduct inventory counts at the end of a period to determine the quantity of finished goods and raw materials on hand. There is different methodology that can be used when placing a value on these quantities

First-in-First-Out Method (FIFO)

This method assumes that inventory that was purchased first was the first to be used in production. Therefore, whatever is remaining on hand at the end of the period was most recently purchased

Last-in-First-Out Method (LIFO)

This method assumes that inventory that was purchased most recently was the first to be used in production. Therefore, whatever is remaining on hand at the end of the period is the oldest inventory purchased.

The LIFO method is rarely used in accounting as it will always result in outdated values of inventory if the entity always inventory on hand at the end of each period.

Weight Average Method

The weighted average method pools the cost of purchases in the period and dividends it by the quantity of purchases to determine an average cost per unit.

This average cost per unit is then applied to the ending quantity to determine the total value of inventory.

EXAMPLE: XYZ Company has the following purchases of materials in the year:

	Quantity	Cost per Unit	Total Cost
January 10	50	$5	$250
May 1	120	$7	$840
September 8	30	$8	$240
December 12	80	$10	$800
Total	280		$2,130

At the end of the year XYZ Company conducts an inventory count and determines they have 110 units of materials on hand.

The value under the three inventory methods would be as follows:

Method	Value	Calculation
FIFO	$1,040	(80 qty x $10 Dec. 12 value) + (30 qty $8 Sept. 12 value)
LIFO	$670	(50 qty x $5 Jan. 12 value) + (60 qty x $7 May 1 Value)
Weighted Avg.	$837	($2,130 total cost / 280 total qty) x 110 qty

Notice how LIFO results in a much higher valuation cost of inventory when prices are rising.

Working Capital

It is important for an entity to ensure they have access to funds to cover their upcoming liabilities. Current assets less current liabilities provide the net working capital of an entity. A negative working capital (current liabilities exceed current access) means an entity will be unable to pay current liabilities at the current moment unless it received cash from other sources.

Non-Current Assets (Debit Accounts)

Long-Term Investments

Investments that are expected to be held longer than a one year period are classified as long-term investments. Examples of long-term investments include long-term bonds with a maturity period of greater than 1 year, stock equities expected to be held longer than 1 year and ownership in other entities.

Short-term and long-term investments are typically valued at fair market value on the balance sheet, so long as they can be readily sold on the open market. Fluctuations in the fair market value of investments are listed as unrealized gains or losses on the income statement. If the investment is listed on an open market the investment is valued at its purchase cost on the balance sheet.

EXAMPLE: XYZ Company purchases 100 shares of ABC Inc. stock (listed on a public stock exchange) on January 13th, 2014 for $90/share in cash. On May 25th, 2014 ABC Inc. stock distributes a $0.25/share dividend. As of May 31, 2014 the stock is trading for $80/share. The company expects to hold on to the investment for a period greater than one year.

The entry to record the initial purchase is as follows:

Date	Account	Debit	Credit
January 13, 2014	Long-Term Investments	$9,000	
January 13, 2014	Cash		$9,000
Total		$9,000	$9,000

The entry to record the dividend is as follows:

Date	Account	Debit	Credit
May 25, 2014	Cash	$25*	
May 25, 2014	Dividend Income		$25
Total		$25	$25

100 shares x $0.25 dividend per share = $25.00

The entry to record the decrease in the value of in the stock price is as follows:

Date	Account	Debit	Credit
May 31, 2014	Unrealized Loss	$1,000*	
May 31, 2014	Long-Term Investments		$1,000
Total		$1,000	$1,000

($80/share - $90/share) x 100 shares = $1,000 Loss

Interest and dividends received from investments are recorded as revenue on the income statement.

Entities often purchase physical assets that will be maintained and used over multiple years. Based on your knowledge of the matching principle you know that items should be expensed in the year in which they are utilized.

Consider a manufacturing plant that acquires machinery and equipment for purpose of producing their product over the next 20 years. To claim the total cost of the machinery in the first year on the income statement would be incorrect given that it will likely be able function for the next 20 years. This is an example of an asset line known as property, plant and equipment, or fixed assets.

Fixed assets are set up on the balance sheet as a long term asset and are reduced via an expense item called amortization or depreciation (the two terms are used interchangeably) over the useful life of the asset. Accumulated depreciation is a contra account to fixed assets and reduces the value of the asset on the balance sheet. Fix assets can be depreciated using the following methods:

1) **Straight-Line Method:** Using the straight line method depreciates the fixed asset evenly throughout its useful life. If an asset was purchased for $100 and had a useful like of 20 years, each year the fixed asset value would be reduced by $5 ($100 / 20 years).

2) **Declining Balance Method:** This method assumes the majority of the benefit of the fixed asset occurs in the first few years; therefore, amortization is weighted heavier at the start and decelerates each year. The following is an amortization schedule of an asset purchased for $1,000 with a declining balance rate of 30% per year:

	Asset Cost	Annual Amortization	Net Book Value
Year 1	$1,000	$300.00	$700.00
Year 2	$1,000	$210.00	$490.00
Year 3	$1,000	$147.00	$343.00
Year 4	$1,000	$102.90	$240.10
Year 5	$1,000	$72.03	$168.07
Year 6	$1,000	$50.42	$117.65

In the first year the amortization is calculated by taking the original cost of the asset ($1,000) and multiplying it by the amortization rate (30%). In year two the amortization is calculated by taking the net book value (cost less accumulated amortization) of the asset at the end of the first year ($700) and multiplying by the amortization rate (30%) which produces an annual amortization of $210 on the asset in the second year. Notice how the amortization continues to decrease year over year now that amortization is based on the net book value of the asset.

Entities often reduce the first year of amortization by 50%. This is called the Half Year Rule. Rarely are all fixed assets purchased at the beginning of the year, therefore, entities may choose to only take 50% of their amortization in year one of the fixed asset.

Entities may choose either method when accounting for fix assets.

Often entities may decide to sell fixed assets resulting in a gain or loss for accounting purposes. More will be discussed on this topic in the income statement chapter.

EXAMPLE: XYZ Company purchases a building on July 14th, 2014 for $400,000 via a bank loan. XYZ has a December 31 year end. The building is expected to last 40 years and XYZ Company amortizes fixed assets using the straight-line method and the half year rule.

The entry to record the initial purchase of the building is:

Date	Account	Debit	Credit
July 14, 2014	Property, Plant & Equipment	$400,000	
July 14, 2014	Bank Loan		$400,000
Total		$400,000	$400,000

At the end of the first year the entry to record the amortization expense is as follows:

Date	Account	Debit	Credit
December 31, 2014	Amortization Expense	$20,000*	
December 31, 2014	Accumulated Amortization		$20,000
Total		$20,000	$20,000

*$400,000 / 40 years x 50% half year rule = $20,000

Improvement VS Repair

Over the life span of a fixed asset an entity may be required to improve or repair the asset.

For accounting purposes improvements are amounts spent which increase the useful life of the fixed asset or improve the operational function of the fixed asset. These types of costs are capitalized (added to the asset book value). Repairs and maintenance of the fixed asset for the purpose of maintenance are expensed directly through the income statement.

In our above building example if XYZ Company purchased a new roof for $10,000 it would need to be determined whether this roof extended the useful life of the building. Assuming the building will last an additional five years, the cost should be added to the book value of the asset.

Intangible Assets

Intangible assets are future benefits controlled by an entity as a result of previous events.

A common example of an intangible asset is the Coca-Cola brand name. Coca-Cola is recognized as a popular soft drink producer around the world and, because of this brand recognition, sells a large amount of product.

Intangible assets can have limited or indefinite lift spans. A trademark is an example of a limited intangible asset as it allows the entity exclusive rights to identify products from a specific source for a set period of time. Intangible assets that are purchased are listed on the balance sheet at their acquisition cost.

Intangible assets can also be generated internally, however, generally accounting standards have moved towards excluding these types of assets.

Short-Term Liabilities (Credit Accounts)

Accounts Payable

An entity is typically invoiced upon receipt of goods and services from an outside party. Accounts payable represent cash or cash consideration owed to suppliers.

Once an invoice is received in the accounting department it will be posted to the accounting system via a journal entry by the accounts payable clerk. The journal entry is a credit to accounts payable and a debit to assets (for a future benefit), liabilities (offsetting another liability) or expense.

Accounts payable are reduced once the entity pays the corresponding invoice. Despite the emergence of electronic payment methods, cheques are often utilized by most large entities to leave a paper trail. A proper paper trail allows an entity to support transactions, which is important when being audited.

Accrued Liabilities

Similar to prepaid expenses, accrued liabilities are a result of the accrual method of accounting. The concept behind accrued liabilities is that expenses within an entity should be recognized in the accounting records in the period the benefit had been incurred regardless of whether it has been paid.

In the above accounts payable section you learned that invoices are posted once received, however, in certain situations invoices may lag behind the related benefit.

EXAMPLE: XYZ Company rents a vehicle from ABC Company starting January 1st, 2014 for a one year term. The total cost of the term rental is $3,000. XYZ has a December 31 year end date.
On February 10th, 2015 ABC Company invoices XYZ Company $3,000 for the rental term.
XYZ Company must accrue this car rental expense at the end of 2014 as follows:

Date	Account	Debit	Credit
December 31, 2014	Rental Expense	$3,000	
December 31, 2014	Accrued Liabilities		$3,000
Total		$3,000	$3,000

When the invoice is received on February 10th, 2015, XYZ Company will make the following entry to reclassify the liability:

Date	Account	Debit	Credit
February 10, 2015	Accrued Liabilities	$3,000	
February 10, 2015	Accounts Payable		$3,000
Total		$3,000	$3,000

If XYZ Company paid the invoice on the same date the entry would be:

Date	Account	Debit	Credit
February 10, 2015	Accounts Payable	$3,000	
February 10, 2015	Cash		$3,000
Total		$3,000	$3,000

In the above example the rental expense is recognized in the year/period it is utilized, rather than the year/period it is invoiced or paid.

Unearned/Deferred Revenue

Deposits are often received by an entity from customers with the expectation that goods or services will be delivered at a later date to the customer. In the previous chapter you learned that revenue recognition requires:

1) **Performance**

2) **Measurability**

3) **Collectability**

It would be premature to record a deposit cash payment as revenue if an entity had not provided goods or services to the customer. For this reason deposits and other upfront payments are recorded as a liability under unearned revenue.

Unearned revenue is recorded as a liability because it represents a future obligation of the entity to provide goods or perform services to a customer for the upfront payment received. This type of liability is the opposite of prepaid expenses discussed earlier in the chapter, where payment is issued from the entity for the rights to future benefits.

Once substantial performance of the obligation to the customer is met the entity may recognize the unearned revenue as revenue.

Bank Loans Payable & Debt

A loan to an entity is an obligation to repay the amount, typically with interest. Payments occur over the term of the loan often blended with both principle and interest. Principle paid represents a decrease in the loan liability and interest is an expense on the income statement.

GAAP requires that an entity separate the loan balance into two separate financial statement lines on the balance sheet:

1) **Current Portion of Long Term Debt:** This line is listed under current assets and contains the principle amount of the loan that will be repaid in the next year.

2) **Long Term Debt:** Is the remaining portion of principle due on the loan that will be paid beyond the one year time period.

EXAMPLE: XYZ Company receives a loan from ABC Bank for $10,000 on January 1st, 2014 for a 5 year loan. Interest is 5% with fixed principle payments of $2,000 each year due December 31 of each year along with interest.

To record the initial loan XYZ Company will book the following journal entry:

Date	Account	Debit	Credit
January 1, 2014	Cash	$10,000	
January 1, 2014	Bank Debt		$10,000
Total		$10,000	$10,000

On December 31st, 2014 XYZ Company will record the following entry:

Date	Account	Debit	Credit
December 31, 2014	Bank Debt	$2,000	
December 31, 2014	Interest Expense	$500*	
December 31, 2014	Cash		$2,500
Total		$2,500	$2,500

Interest: $10,000 loan x 5% interest rate = $500

At the end of 2014 XYZ Company would classify their bank loan on the balance sheet under liabilities as follows:

Current Liabilities	
Current Portion of Long-Term Debt	$2,000*
Long-Term Liabilities	
Long-Term Debt	$6,000
TOTAL LIABILITIES	$8,000

The current portion of long term debt is the $2,000 of principle that will be due at the end of 2015.

When discussing the balance sheet equation it was determined equity is the net value of the company. For financial statement presentation purposes equity is listed on the balance sheet, or as a separate statements called the statement of equity. If an entity is incorporated equity is referred to as shareholder equity. Equity can be generated or reduced internally and externally.

Internal

Retained Earnings

As discussed in the previous chapter net income or loss is revenue less expenses for the entity in a given period. Once the period has finished this income or loss is transferred to retained earnings at the beginning of the next period.

Retained earnings are accumulated throughout the life of an entity and will be reflected by an increase in assets.

Corporate Dividends

Corporations are legally entities that are owned by a shareholder. In order to pay a shareholder out retained earnings (profit) from the corporation a payment referred to as a dividend is issued.

Corporations may have one single shareholder (owns 100% of the corporation) or thousands of shareholders (public companies that are listed on a stock exchange are an example). Dividends directly reduce retained earnings.

External:

Common Stock (Corporation)

Common stock represents ownership of a corporation. Owners of stock in corporations are referred to as shareholders. This ownership can be sold to other individuals or held indefinitely.

When a corporation issues stock to shareholders it typically receives cash or consideration in exchange – this increases the value of corporation.

Preferred Stock (Corporation)

Preferred stock is also an ownership in a corporation; however, it has different qualities than common stock. Preferred shareholders have a right to dividends before common shareholders receive their dividend. In exchange for this preferable treatment preferred shareholders typically give up rights to additional dividend payments for increased earnings if issued by the corporation to common shareholders.

EXAMPLE: On January 1st, 2014 XYZ Company, an incorporated entity in its first year of operations, issues 100 common shares to the public for $5 each and 100 preferred shares for $6 each with a stated dividend of $1.00 per share.

For the year ending December 31, 2014 XYZ Company records a $1,000 net income and declares a $2 per share dividend on common stock.

To record the initial sales of stock XYZ Company would record the following entry:

Date	Account	Debit	Credit
January 1, 2014	Cash	$1,100	
January 1, 2014	Common Stock (Equity)		$500*
January 1, 2014	Preferred Stock (Equity)		$600**
Total		$1,100	$1,100

*Common Stock: 100 shares x $5/share = $500 **Preferred Stock: 100 shares x $6/share = $600*

To record the declaration of dividends at the end of the year XYZ would record the following entry:

Date	Account	Debit	Credit
December 31, 2014	Dividends on Common Stock	$200	
December 31, 2014	Dividends on Preferred Stock	$100	
December 31, 2014	Dividends Payable (Liability)		$300
Total		$1,100	$1,100

At the end of the year XYZ Company would report the following statement of shareholders' equity:

XYZ Company	

Statement of Shareholders' Equity	
For the year ended December 31, 2014	
Opening Balance	$0
Issue of Common Share	$500
Issue of Preferred Shares	$600
Net Income	$1,000
Dividends	($300)
Ending Balance	$1,800

Comprehensive Balance Sheet Example

XYZ Company is a corporation that had the following transactions in its first year of operations which ended December 31st, 2014:

1) Sold 500 common shares for $5 per share on January 10th 2014 in cash

2) The company purchased a bond on January 1st, 2014 maturing in one year for $5,000 bearing 4% interest that is paid on December 31st, 2014

3) Acquired a cash loan from the bank of $100,000 on April 8th, 2014 bearing 6% annual interest with first payment not due until April 8th, 2016

4) Purchased operating insurance on January 3rd, 2014 for January 1, 2014 to December 15th, 2015 for $5,000 in cash

5) Purchased manufacturing equipment for $5,000 that is expected to last 10 years on May 10th, 2014

6) Purchased a building for $80,000 that is expected to last 40 years on May 12th, 2014

7) Gross accounts receivable at year end were $30,000 which represents total sales for the year

8) Accounts payable at the end of the year were $8,000

9) On December 10th, 2014 manufacturing equipment owned by the corporation failed and had to be repaired immediately for $3,000. The

corporation did not receive an invoice by December 31st, 2014 for the above repair

10) A dividend of $3 per share was declared for December 31, 2014 but not yet paid out

Assumptions for XYZ Company:

1) The percentage of receivables method is used to estimate allowance for bad debt using a rate of 10%

2) Straight-line method and half year rule is used when calculating amortization

Journal Entries Required

1) Sale of common shares:

Date	Account	Debit	Credit
January 10, 2014	Cash	$2,500	
January 10, 2014	Common Stock		$2,500
Total		$2,500	$2,500

2) Bond purchase:

Date	Account	Debit	Credit
January 1, 2014	Short-Term Investments	$5,000	
January 1, 2014	Cash		$5,000
Total		$5,000	$5,000

3) Bank loan received:

Date	Account	Debit	Credit
April 8, 2014	Cash	$100,000	
April 8, 2014	Long-Term Debt		$100,000
Total		$100,000	$100,000

4) Insurance premium paid:

Date	Account	Debit	Credit
January 3, 2014	Prepaid Expenses	$5,000	

January 3, 2014	Cash		$5,000
Total		$5,000	$5,000

5) Purchase of manufacturing equipment:

Date	Account	Debit	Credit
May 10, 2014	Property, Plant & Equipment	$5,000	
May 10, 2014	Cash		$5,000
Total		$5,000	$5,000

6) Purchase of building:

Date	Account	Debit	Credit
May 12, 2014	Property, Plant & Equipment	$80,000	
May 12, 2014	Cash		$80,000
Total		$80,000	$80,000

7) Accounts receivable entry:

Date	Account	Debit	Credit
December 31, 2014	Accounts Receivable	$30,000	
December 31, 2014	Sales		$30,000
Total		$30,000	$30,000

8) Accounts payable entry:

Date	Account	Debit	Credit
December 31, 2014	Income Statement Expense	$8,000	
December 31, 2014	Accounts Payable		$8,000
Total		$8,000	$8,000

9) Repair of equipment not yet paid or invoiced but benefit received:

Date	Account	Debit	Credit
December 31, 2014	Repairs and Maintenance	$3,000	
December 31, 2014	Accrued Liabilities		$3,000
Total		$3,000	$3,000

10) Dividends declared:

Date	Account	Debit	Credit
December 31, 2014	Dividends Declared	$1,500	
December 31, 2014	Dividends Payable		$1,500
Total		$1,500	$1,500

11) Yearend adjusting entry for amortization:

Date	Account	Debit	Credit
December 31, 2014	Amortization Expense	$1,250	
December 31, 2014	Accumulated Amortization		$250*
December 31, 2014	Accumulated Amortization		$1,000**
Total		$1,250	$1,250

*Amortization on equipment: $5,000 cost / 10 years useful life x 50% half year = $250
**Amortization on building: $80,000 cost / 40 years useful life x 50% half year = $1,000

12) Yearend adjusting entry for prepaid expense on insurance:

Date	Account	Debit	Credit
December 31, 2014	Insurance Expense	$2,500*	
December 31, 2014	Prepaid Expense		$2,500
Total		$2,500	$2,500

*Amortization of prepaid insurance: $5,000 cost x ½ utilized = $2,500

13) Year end adjusting entry for allowance for bad debts:

Date	Account	Debit	Credit
December 31, 2014	Bad Debt Expense	$3,000*	
December 31, 2014	Allowance for Bad Debts		$3,000
Total		$3,000	$3,000

*Bad debt expense: $30,000 gross receivables x 10% rate = $3,000

14) Interest received on short-term investments:

Date	Account	Debit	Credit
December 31, 2014	Cash	$200*	
December 31, 2014	Interest Revenue		$200
Total		$200	$200

Bond interest: $5,000 x 4% interest = $250

15) Accrued interest on bank loan:

Date	Account	Debit	Credit
December 31, 2014	Interest Expense	$4,398.04	
December 31, 2014	Accrued Liabilities		$4,398.04
Total		$4,398.04	$4,398.04

Accrued interest: $100,000 loan x 6% x 267/365 days (April 8th – December 31st) = $4,389.04

Adding up all the account transactions provides the following trial balance:

XYZ Company			
Trial Balance			
As at December 31, 2014			
Account	**Debit**	**Credit**	**Statement**
Cash	7,700.00		Balance Sheet
Accounts Receivable	30,000.00		Balance Sheet
Allowance for Bad Debts		3,000.00	Balance Sheet
Short-Term Investments	5,000.00		Balance Sheet
Prepaid Expenses	2,500.00		Balance Sheet
Property, Plant & Equipment	85,000.00		Balance Sheet
Accumulated Amortization		1,250.00	Balance Sheet
Accounts Payable		8,000.00	Balance Sheet
Dividends Payable		1,500.00	Balance Sheet
Accrued Liabilities		7,389.04	Balance Sheet
Long-Term Debt		100,000.00	Balance Sheet
Common Stock		2,500.00	Balance Sheet
Dividends Declared	1,500.00		Balance Sheet
Interest Revenue		200.00	Income Statement
Sales		30,000.00	Income Statement
Amortization Expense	1,250.00		Income Statement
Bad Debt Expense	3,000.00		Income Statement
Income Statement Expense	8,000.00		Income Statement
Insurance Expense	2,500.00		Income Statement
Interest Expense	4,389.04		Income Statement
Repairs and Maintenance	3,000.00		Income Statement
	153,839.04	153,839.04	

The balance sheet for XYZ Company:

XYZ Company		
Balance Sheet		
As at December 31, 2014		
ASSETS		
Current Assets:		
Cash	$7,700	
Accounts Receivable, Net	27,000	*Includes allowance for bad debt*
Short-Term Investments	5,000	
Prepaid Expenses	25,000	*Gross cost less amortization*
	42,000	
Long-Term Assets:		
Property, Plant & Equipment	83,750	
TOTAL ASSETS	**$125,950**	
LIABILITIES		
Current Liabilities:		
Accounts Payable	$8,000	
Accrued Liabilities	7,389	
Dividends Payable	1,500	
	16,869	
Long-Term Liabilities:		
Bank Loan	100,000	*Payment not due until 2016, therefore all long term*
TOTAL LIABILITIES	$116,889	
SHAREHOLDERS' EQUITY		
Common Stock	$2,500	
Retained Earnings	8,061	*Summation of income statement accounts from trial balance*
Dividends Declared	(1,500)	
	$9,061	
TOTAL LIABILITIES &	**$125,950**	

The above example reviews the transactions that were reviewed in throughout this chapter. While the volume of transactions for most entities is much higher in a given year, it represents the building blocks of any balance sheet and the required presentation.

In the next chapter you will learn how an entity accounts for profit and loss on the income statement.

Chapter 3 Summary

- The balance sheet is a snapshot of an entities financial position at a specific time

- The balance sheet consists of assets (benefits of an entity), liabilities (sacrifices of an entity) and equity (value of an entity)

- Assets and liabilities are classified as current if they can be liquidated or paid within a one year period

- Assets and liabilities are classified as long-term if they will not be paid or liquidated within a one year period

- Property, plant and equipment are listed on the balance sheet at their net book value (acquisition cost less accumulated depreciation)

- Equity can be generated internally via net income or externally via cash infusions from investors

Chapter 4
Income Statement

The income statement is a summary of the operations of an entity over a period of specified time.

An income statement title lists the name of the entity, the type of statement and the report date of the statement. For example:

XYZ Company (Company)
Income Statement (Statement Type)
For the year ending December 31, 20XX (Report Date)

From a previous chapter you learned the income statement equation:
NET INCOME = REVENUE - EXPENSES

We will now look at the various components that make up revenue and expenses.

Revenue

In chapter 2 you learned that revenue is income generated by an entity and has specific criteria that must be met before it is recorded (revenue recognition).

Sales Revenue

Sales revenue is income the entity generates via its product or service offering. Typically this is reported on one financial statement line; however, there may multiple sales revenue accounts to track the sales volume for different products or services within the entity.

Interest Revenue

An entity may receive interest from banks on bank accounts balances or from different types of investments held.

Dividend Revenue

Amounts received from shares held in investments or other corporations

Royalty Revenue

An entity may have the rights to certain assets that it allows other organizations to use for a fee, known as royalties. For example, a McDonald's restaurant owner must pay royalty fees to the McDonald's Corporation.

Expenses

Cost of Goods Sold

Cost of goods sold are expenses incurred to directly produce revenue. Manufacturing organizations are good examples of entities that spend a large portion of their overall expenses on cost of goods sold. In chapter 3 you learned finished goods are comprised of:

1) **Direct Materials**
2) **Direct Labour:**
3) **Variable & Fixed Overheads**

Once a finished good is sold to a customer it is moved from assets on the balance sheet to cost of goods sold. To calculate the total cost of goods sold in a given period the following calculation is used:

Cost of Goods Sold = (Beginning Inventory) + (Purchases) – (Ending Inventory)

In the above equation inventory is the balance of finished goods on the balance sheet and purchases are the inputs of direct materials, direct labour and variable & fixed overheads.

EXAMPLE: XYZ Company begins the fiscal year with $12,000 in finished goods. Throughout the year the company spends $50,000 on direct materials, $80,000 on direct labour and $40,000 in overhead. At the end of the fiscal year XYZ company has $20,000 of finished goods on hand.

XYZ would calculate their cost of goods sold for the year as follows:

Beginning Balance – Finished Goods		$12,000.00
Purchases:		
Direct Materials	$50,000.00	
Direct Labour	$80,000.00	
Overheads	$4,000.00	$134,000.00

Ending Balance – Finished Goods	($20,000.00)
Total Cost of Goods Sold	$126,000.00

Selling, General and Administrative

Expenses listed under selling, general and administrative are fixed costs associated with operating the entity, excluding costs associated with producing the product. The term fixed cost in accounting refers to expenditures that are set regardless of the production level. Think of an entity that pays administrative staff to manage the accounting department; even if the entity failed to produce or sell product the entity must pay the accounting department.

Selling costs are expenditures incurred for the purpose of retailing an entities products or services. Typical expenditures in selling costs include sales salaries, commissions and advertising and promotion.

General and administrative costs are overheads relating to managing the overall business. Examples of general and administrative include legal fees, accounting fees, administrative salaries, insurance, office rent and supplies.

Amortization/Depreciation

You learned in chapter 3 that amortization or depreciation is the method in which property, plant and equipment is expensed to the income statement. This is done to comply with the matching principle that requires an entity to expense assets/benefits in the period it is utilized.

For financial statement presentation purposes amortization is presented on one line item; however, it typically contains multiple amortization accounts to allow each property, plant and equipment class to be amortized separately based on its useful life (amortization rate).

EXAMPLE: XYZ Company purchases a building for $100,000, manufacturing equipment for $50,000 and a vehicle for $20,000. The company uses the following method for amortizing its property, plant and equipment:

- Building: 10% declining balance method

- Manufacturing: 30% declining balance method

- Vehicle: 5 year straight-line method

- No half year rule

To record amortization for the year XYZ Company would use the following calculations:

Building Amortization ($100,000 x 10%)	$10,000.00
Manufacturing Amortization ($50,000 x 30%)	$15,000.00
Vehicle Amortization ($20,000 / 5 years)	$4,000.00
Total	$19,000.00

Non-Operating Section

Transactions that are not in the normal course of an entity's operations are presented in a separate area on the income statement. This is separated so that the main operations of a business can be distinguished from one-time transactions.

Realized and Unrealized Gains/(Losses) on Investments

In chapter 3 you learned that investments are adjusted and carried at their fair market value on the balance sheet. The other side of the adjustment is to the income statement under unrealized gains or losses. In order to be carried at fair market value the investment should be readily sellable on an open market.

When investments are sold the difference between the initial acquisition cost and selling price is recorded as a realized gain or loss.

EXAMPLE: XYZ Company purchases 200 public shares of ABC Corporation, a publically listed corporation, for $20 each on April 13th, 2014. At the end of XYZ Company's fiscal year, December 31st, 2014, they are still holding the shares that are now selling for $30 per share on the stock exchange.

To record this increase in value XYZ Company will post the following journal entry:

Date	Account	Debit	Credit
December 31, 2014	Investments	*$2,000.00	
December 31, 2014	Unrealized Gain		$2,000.00
Total		$2,000.00	$2,000.00

*($30 per share - $20 per share) x 200 shares

On January 5th, 2015, XYZ Company sells the shares for $32 per share and records the following entry:

Date	Account	Debit	Credit
January 5, 2015	Cash	*$6,400.00	
January 5, 2015	Unrealized Gain	$2,000.00	
January 5, 2015	Realized Gain		$2,000.00
January 5, 2015	Realized Gain		**$400.00
January 5, 2015	Investments		$6,000.00
Total		$8,400.00	$8,400.00

*200 shares x $32 each
**200 shares x ($32 sell price - $30 valuation)

Gain/(Loss) on Sales of Property, Plant and Equipment

An entity may sell property, plant and equipment to outside parties which may generate a gain or loss on the income statement. The gain or loss is calculated by subtracting the net book value from the selling price of the asset. Recall from chapter 3 net book value is the acquisition cost of the asset less accumulated depreciation. Therefore the expanded calculation for the gain or loss is as follows:

Selling Price - (Acquisition Cost – Accumulated Amortization) = Gain/(Loss)

Gains or losses resulted from the sale of fixed assets are presented on a separate line item away from revenue as these types of transactions are not in the normal course of an entity's business.

EXAMPLE: Using the scenario from the amortization example earlier in the chapter XYZ Company would have the following value of property, plant and equipment:

Asset Class	Book Value	Accum. Amortization	Net Book Value
Building	$100,000.00	$10,000.00	$90,000.00
Equipment	$50,000.00	$15,000.00	$35,000.00
Vehicle	$20,000.00	$4,000.00	$16,000.00

If XYZ Company sold their equipment for $40,000 the following entry would be required to book the gain on the sale:

Account	Debit	Credit
Cash	$40,000.00	
Accumulated Amortization	$15,000.00	
Equipment		$50,000.00
Gain on Sale		$5,000.00

The above entry clears the prior accumulated amortization booked on the equipment as well as the acquisition cost of the equipment. The $5,000 gain on the sale is the sales price ($40,000) less the net book value ($35,000).

Income Taxes

Income taxes are typically the last item before net income on an income statement. This item represents amounts owed to governments on profits earned within the entity for the period. Each country has its own specific tax laws which entities must comply with.

Comprehensive Income Statement Example

XYZ Company has the following transactions for the year ended December 31, 2014:

1) Product revenue of $400,000 all received in cash

2) Opening finished goods inventory of $40,000

3) Purchases of direct materials were $50,000

4) Direct wages paid were $70,000

5) Variable and fixed overhead of $30,000

6) Purchased 300 common stock shares in ABC Company on May 2nd, 2014 for $15 each

7) Paid commissions to marketing companies totalling $5,000

8) Consumed $6,000 in office supplies

9) Paid $100,000 to office administrative staff

10) Made no purchases of property, plant and equipment but at the beginning of the year had net book values of $250,000 and $100,000 for building and equipment, respectively

11) Sold 100 shares of ABC Company stock for $12 each

12) Received $2 per share dividend from ABC stock on the remaining 200 common shares held

13) Finished goods inventory at the end of the year was $30,000

14) ABC Company was trading for $16 per share at the end of the year

Assumptions:

1) XYZ Company uses the declining balance method to record amortization. Building rate is 10% and equipment rate is 20%

2) XYZ Company has a corporate tax rate of 20%

XYZ Company has the following income statement:

Income Statement		
XYZ Company		
For the period Ending December 31, 2014		
Revenue	$400,000	
Cost of Goods Sold	160,000	Note 1
Gross Margin	$240,000	
General , Selling and Administrative Expenses:		
Administrative Wages	$100,000	
Commissions	$5,000	
Office Supplies	$6,000	
	$111,000	
Amortization Expense	45,000	Note 2

Operating Income	$84,000	$240,000 - $111,000 – $45,000
Other Income and Expenses:		
Dividend Income	$400	$2 per share x 200 shares
Realized Gain/(Loss) on Sale of Investments	($300)	
Unrealized Gain/(Loss) on Sale of Investments	$200	
	$300	
Income before Taxes	$84,300	$84,000 + $300
Income Tax Expense	$16,860	$84,300 x 20% tax rate
Net Income	**$67,440**	$84,300 - $16,860

Note 1) Cost of goods sold is calculated as follows:

Opening Inventory	$40,000.00
Purchases:	
Direct Materials	$50,000.00
Direct Wages	$70,000.00
Overheads	$30,000.00
Ending Inventory	($30,000)
Total Cost of Goods Sold	$160,000.00

Note 2) Amortization expense is calculated as follows:

Building Amortization ($250,000 x 10%)	$25,000.00
Equipment Amortization ($100,000 x 20%)	$20,000.00
Total	$45,000.00

Chapter 4 Summary

- The income statement provides a summary of profitability of an entity for a given time period

- Gross margin is calculated as revenue minus cost of goods sold

- Cost of goods sold = Beginning Inventory + Purchases − Ending Inventory

- Purchases are direct materials, direct wages and overhead

- General, sells and administrative expenses are costs required to run the overall business but not to produce actual products or services

- Income or expenses not in the usual course of operation for an entity are reported separately from operating income

- Income taxes are the last expense item on the income statement that is calculated by taking income before income taxes multiplied by the applicable tax rate

Chapter 5
Statement of Cash Flows

The purpose of the statement of cash flows is to present the entity's capacity to generate cash as well as the entity's needs for cash. Knowing how the company earns and spends cash is important to users of the financial statement because cash is the life line of an entity. Similar to the income statement, this statement represents transactions of a given time period.

Creditors would closely examine the cash flow statement of an entity to determine the entity's ability to pay back a loan. It is a good sign if the entity is consistently generating positive cash flows from the primary course of business.

Sections of the Statement of Cash Flows

The statement of cash flows is broken down into three sourced classifications; operating activities, investment activities and financing activities.

Operating Activities

In chapter 4 you learned that operating income is the profit earned from an entity's normal course of business. Cash flow from operating activities represent cash in and out from the principle revenue producing operations.

This section of the cash flow statement begins with net income of an entity and is adjusted for all non-cash items.

Cash changes from operating activities include:

- Increase in cash for net income

- Decrease in cash for increases in the account receivable account (accounts receivable represent net income generated on credit not cash)

- Increase in cash for increases in accounts payable

- Decrease in cash for increases in prepaid expenses

- Amortization expense is an increase in cash as it is an expense that does not involve cash

- Income tax expense is an increase in cash as it does not involve cash

Cash earned or spent on investments that are not in the normal course of operations are listed under investing activities. The sale of external common shares or bonds would be listed under this classification.

Cash changes from investing activities include:

- Decrease in cash for property, plant and equipment

- Decrease in cash for purchase of investments

- Increase in cash for the sale of property, plant and equipment and investments

Financing Activities

Financing activities are cash flows received or spent for the purposes of funding the entity. In the classification a loan from the bank would be listed as a cash inflow and principle and debt repayments on the debt would be listed as a cash outflow.

Cash changes from financing activities include:

- Increase in cash for loans received

- Decrease in cash for principle and interest loan repayment

- Increase in cash for sale of equity (common and preferred shares)

- Decrease in cash for dividends issued to shareholders

Comprehensive Statement of Cash Flow Example

XYZ Company has the following transactions for their **first** fiscal year ending December 31, 2014:

1) Net income for the year of $300,000

2) Amortization expense of $50,000

3) Income tax expense of $75,000

4) Ending accounts payable balance of $20,000

5) Ending accounts receivable balance of $45,000
6) Ending prepaid expense balance of $10,000

7) Acquired a bank loan for $350,000

8) Made principle and interest repayments of $65,000 on the bank loan

9) Purchased property, plant and equipment of $150,000

10) Issued 2,000 common shares of corporate stock for $20 per share

11) Paid dividends of $1.50 per share on common shares

Statement of Cash Flows		
XYZ Company		
For the period Ending December 31, 2014		
Cash Provided by (Used in):		
OPERATIONS:		
Net Income	$300,000	
Items not affecting cash:		
Amortization	$50,000	
Income Tax	$75,000	
Changes in Working Capital	($35,000)	Note 1
Cash Provided by Operations	$390,000	
INVESTMENTS:		
Expenditures on Property, Plant and Equipment	($150,000)	
FINANCING:		
Proceeds from Bank Loan	$350,000	
Repayments of Bank Loan	($65,000)	
Proceeds from Issuance of Common Shares	$40,000	2,000 shares x $20/share
Dividends Paid	($3,000)	2,000 shares x $1.50/share

Cash Provided by Financing	$378,000	
Increase in Cash and Cash Equivalents	$618,000	$390,000 - $150,000 + $378,000
Cash and Cash Equivalents, beginning of year	$-	
Cash and Cash Equivalents, end of year	$618,000	

Note 1) Changes in working capital is calculated as follows:

Increase in Accounts Payable	$20,000
Increase in Accounts Receivable	($45,000)
Increase in Prepaid Expenses	($10,000)
	($35,000)

Chapter 5 Summary

- The statement of cash flows shows the cash generated and cash requirements of an entity for a given period of time

- The three classifications of changes in cash on the statement of cash flows are operations, financing and investments

- Cash flows generated by the operations within an entity is a positive sign that the entity is capable of producing cash from its main course of business

- Cash is the life line of an entity

Chapter 6
Financial Analysis and Ratios

Financial statements present a large amount of information to users of the statements. It is the responsibility of the users of the financial statements to analyze the information in such a way that allows them to make informed decisions on the current and future performance of an entity.

In order to identify financial risks and opportunities within an entity users of the financial statements use financial analysis and ratios to assist in determining these risks and opportunities.

Comparative Analysis

A comparative analysis in financial accounting identifies trends in an organization by paralleling similar information over different time periods. This analysis can be used to identify trends and developments within an organization.

Most financial statements include a column for the current period results as well as a column for the previous period results each period covering the same time frame. This allows the user of the financial statements to observe the change in the financial position of the organization in the current period.

Liquidity Ratios

In chapter 3 you learned that net working capital showed the ability of an entity to cover its current liabilities for the current period. Liquidity ratios provide a further analysis of an entity's short-run ability to pay its upcoming obligations

Current Ratio

Formula: (Current Assets) / (Current Liabilities)

The current ratio looks at the current benefits/assets and obligations/liabilities of an entity. Recall that current assets and current liabilities are items that will be liquidated within a one year period. A healthy entity will have a minimum ratio of 1:1 which means once the current assets are liquidated they will be able to pay their obligations.

Quick or Acid-Test Ratio

Formula: (Cash + Short-Term Investments + Net Receivables) / (Current Liabilities)

The quick ratio alters the above current ratio by including only assets that can easily be liquidated in an entity. This ratio is more conservative than the current ratio because it looks at asset items that are already liquidated (cash) and items that can quickly be liquidated (short-term investments and receivables). A very healthy entity will have a ratio exceeding 1:1.

Current Cash Debt Coverage Ratio

Formula: (Net Cash Provided by Operating Activities) / (Averaged Current Liabilities)

In chapter 5 you learned that cash provided by operating activities showed the ability of an entity to generate cash via its primary business operations. The current cash debt ratio compares the cash generated from the primary business operations to the average current liabilities of an entity. Averaged current liabilities is calculated by taking opening current liabilities adding ending current liabilities and dividing by two.

When cash from operating activities exceeds the average current liabilities the entity is able to pay its short-term obligations with cash generated internally.

Activity Ratios

Management of an entity strive to utilize assets to generate income. Activity ratios measure the efficiency in which the entity deploys its assets as well as how quickly the entity is able to turn inventory and receivables into cash.

Receivable Turnover

Formula: (Net Sales) / (Average Net Trade Receivables)

It is useful to know how quickly an entity generates cash from receivables. The higher the receivable turnover ratio the faster an entity collects cash from its customers. An entity with a very low receivable turnover ratio means they are slower at collecting from customers, which is more risky.

Average net trade receivables are the opening and closing balance of customer accounts receivable divided by two.

Inventory Turnover

Formula: (Cost of Goods Sold) / (Average Finished Goods Inventory)

Inventory turnover measures the ability of an entity to turn inventory into sales. It is consider positive if an entity has a high inventory turnover ratio as it indicates the entity is quickly turning its inventory into revenue.

Asset Turnover

Formula: (Net Sales) / (Average Total Assets)

The asset turnover ratio calculates the efficiency in which assets generate sales. If an entity has a low asset turnover it means assets are stagnant and not being used efficiently.

Profitability Ratios

The objective of most entities is to generate profit. Looking at the net income may not always provide the correct context for an investor making decisions because it can be a relative figure. For example, suppose Company A generated $100 of net income deploying $300 of assets and Company B generated $50 of net income deploying $100 of assets. While Company A generated a higher dollar figure of net income, Company B utilized its net assets in a more efficient manner generating $0.50 of net income ($50/$100) for each dollar of assets compared to Company A that generated only $0.30 of net income ($100/$300) for each dollar of assets. If the same ratio held true as assets increased a wise investor would choose to invest in Company B.

Profit Margin on Sales

Formula: (Net Income) / (Net Sales)

The profit margin on sales ratio measures the net income generated by each dollar of sales. This metric is useful to determine the efficiency of operations within an entity when generating net income.

Rate of Return on Assets

Formula: (Net Income) / (Average Total Assets)

Assets are used in an entity to generate revenue. The efficiency that these assets are utilized is measured in the rate of return on assets. The example of the beginning of the profit margin ratios compared Company A versus Company B and using the rate of return on total assets we determined Company B was the better investment option, all else held equal, because return on total assets. This ratio is useful to managers in determining the optimal amount of assets to produce the desired net income.

Earnings per Share

Formula: (Net Income) / (Shares Outstanding)

Investors typically measure a corporation by the earnings per share to determine their piece of the profitability of the corporation. If Corporation A has net income of $1,000 and 2,000 shares outstanding the earnings per share would be $0.50 ($1,000 / 2,000 shares).

This metric can be misleading at times when comparing earnings per share of different corporations because it does not take into consideration the amount investors paid to obtain shares. Earnings per share is most useful when combined with the next ratio discuss – price earnings ratio.

Price Earnings Ratio

Formula: (Market Price of Shares) / (Earnings per Share)

The price earnings ratio builds on the earnings per share metric by consider the cost of acquiring shares in the corporation. By using the market price of the shares in the calculation it is possible to see the cost associated to the investor to earn net income in the corporation. Using our above example of Corporation A that had earnings per share of $0.50 let us assume the current market value of one share in Corporation A is $12. The price earnings ratio of Corporation A is 24 ($12 / $0.50). Essentially what this means is an investor would be required to pay $24 to earn $1 of net income in Corporation A.

This metric is useful when comparing companies in similar industries. Typically entities within the same industry would be expected to have similar price earnings ratios.

Payout Ratio

Formula: (Cash Dividends) / (Net Income)

The payout ratio measures the percentage of earnings paid out to investors in a given period. Essentially a corporation has two decisions when determining what to do with net income 1) Reinvest the earnings back in the corporation 2) Pay dividends out to investors.

Some corporations choose to pay very little or no dividends to shareholders, instead opting to the earnings back into the business in order to grow. Cash payments in the form of dividends are always welcomed by investors but investors also want to see the value of their held shares grow.

Coverage Ratios

At the beginning of this chapter you looked at liquidity ratios, which provides a means to analyze the short-term funding of obligations in an entity. Coverage ratios look further down the road and take into consideration long-term liabilities and an entity's ability to meet them.

Debt to Total Assets

Formula: (Total Debt) / (Total Assets)

The debt to total assets ratio measures the total assets of entity provided by outside debt. A company with a high debt to total assets ratio is considered to be highly leveraged. Being a highly leveraged entity presents a higher degree of risk because more cash must be generated in the business to pay its obligations and avoid being in default with creditors.

Cash Debt Coverage Ratio

Formula: (Net Cash Provided by Operating Activities) / (Average Total Liabilities)

The cash debt coverage ratio looks at the percentage of creditor obligations that can be paid with cash from the normal course of business operations. In chapter 5 you learned the first part on the statement of cash flows was cash provided by operating activities, which is net income adjusted for any non-cash transactions. An entity that has a cash debt coverage ratio below 1 would be unable to pay off to pay off their creditor obligations with cash earned from the normal course of business in the given year. The higher this ratio the more likely the entity will be able to continue paying down debt and liabilities in future years to come.

Book Value per Share

Formula: (Shareholders' Equity) / (Outstanding Shares)

Using the balance sheet equation you know that shareholders' equity is equal to total assets less total liabilities. The book value per share ratio measures the amount investors would receive if the entity was liquidated.

Consider an entity that recently came into a default position and could no longer pay creditors and operate. Government agencies would require the entity to file for bankruptcy and liquidate all assets. Once the assets were liquidated the various creditors would be paid the amounts owed. Only after creditors are paid would investors receive compensation for their shares. If the company was unable to pay all creditors with the liquidation of assets then the investors would receive nothing. This is not an unusual situation when large corporations file for bankruptcy.

Comprehensive Financial Analysis and Ratio Example

Income Statement		
XYZ Company		
For the period Ending December 31, 2015		
	2015	**2014**
Revenue	$350,000	$400,000
Cost of Goods Sold	150,000	160,000
Gross Margin	200,000	240,000
General , Selling and Administrative Expenses		
Administrative Wages	90,000	100,000
Commissions	4,000	5,000
Office Supplies	7,000	6,000
	101,000	111,000
Amortization Expense	43,000	45,000
Operating Income	56,000	84,000

Other Income and Expenses:		
Dividend Income	$250	400
Realized Gain/(Loss) on Sale of Investments	-	(300)
Unrealized Gain/(Loss) on Investments	-	200
	250	300
Income before Taxes	56,250	84,300
Income Tax Expense	11,250	16,860
Net Income	**$45,000**	**$67,440**

Let's assume XYZ Company has the following corresponding balance sheet for the same time period:

XYZ Company		
Balance Sheet		
As at December 31, 2015		
	2015	**2014**
ASSETS		
Current Assets:		
Cash	$1,250	$2,241
Accounts Receivable, Net	90,000	80,000
Short-Term Investments	3,000	3,200
Inventory – Raw Materials	15,000	10,000
Inventory – Finished Goods	50,000	40,000
	159,250	135,441
Long-Term Assets:		
Property, Plant & Equipment	350,000	305,000
TOTAL ASSETS	**$509,250**	**$440,441**
LIABILITIES		
Current Liabilities:		
Accounts Payable	63,460	$56,000
Accrued Liabilities	40,000	15,000
Current Portion of Long-Term Debt	4,000	3,000
	107,460	74,000

Long-Term Liabilities:		
Bank Loan	290,000	300,000
TOTAL LIABILITIES	397,460	374,000
SHAREHOLDERS' EQUITY		
Common Stock	100	100
Retained Earnings	112,440	67,440
Dividends Declared on 100 Common Shares	(750)	(900)
	111,790	66,441
TOTAL LIABILITIES & SHAREHOLDERS' EQUITY	**$509,250**	**$440,441**

Current Ratio

2015: (159,250 Current Assets) / ($107,460 Current Liabilities) = 1.48
2014: ($135,441 Current Assets) / ($74,000 Current Liabilities) = 1.83

Despite a decrease in the ratio from 2014 to 2015, XYZ Company still has current assets exceeding current liabilities. This means that XYZ Company is expecting to liquidate more than enough assets in the next year to cover the upcoming obligations within the year.

Quick Ratio

2015: ($1,250 Cash + $90,000 Accounts Receivable + $3,000 short-Term Investments) / ($107,460 Current Liabilities) = 0.88
2014: ($2,241 Cash + $80,000 Accounts Receivable + $3,200 Short-Term Investments) / ($74,000 Current Liabilities) = 1.15

The quick ratio is a more conservative liquidity ratio than the current ratio as it excludes non-cash items such as inventory, prepaid expenses and other current assets. XYZ Company's quick ratio fell below one in 2015 as current liabilities increased at a higher rate than cash, accounts receivable and short-term investments.

Current Cash Debt Coverage Ratio

To determine this ratio we first have to calculate the net cash from operations as follows:

	2015	2014

Operating Income	56,000	$84,440
Items Not Affecting Cash:		
Amortization	43,000	45,000
Change in Working Capital	(9,651)	61,441
Total Cash From Operations	$89,349	$190,881

2015: ($89,349 Cash from Operations / $90,730 Average Current Liabilities) = 0.98
2014: ($190,881 Cash from Operations / ($37,000 Average Current Liabilities) = 5.16

To calculate the average current liabilities in 2014 we will assume this is the first year of operations for XYZ Company, so the average is equal to $74,000 / 2. In 2015 we have an opening balance for current liabilities (closing balance in 2014 of $74,000); therefore, the calculation for average current liabilities in 2015 is calculated as ($107,460 + $74,000) / 2 = $90,730.

The ratio calculated in 2014 is misleading because this was the first year in which XYZ Company operated and no opening balance for liabilities existed. The 2015 ratio of 0.98 is more accurate given that it includes a normal opening and closing balance of liabilities.

Receivable Turnover

2015: ($350,000 Net Sales) / ($85,000 Average Receivables) = 4.12
2014: ($400,000 Net Sales) / ($40,000 Average Receivables) = 10.00

A receivable turnover of 4.12 means that XYZ Company collected their total receivable balances 4.12 times in 2015. Again, the 2014 ratio is misleading because of understated average receivables due to the first year of operations.

A more useful metric is taking the number of days in the year and dividing it by the receivable turnover of 4.12, which will give us 88.59. This calculation is known as the average days of sales in receivables and tells us how long on average it took XYZ Company to collect balances from customers. This figure assists management in determine credit terms with customers. In 2015 customers were paying XYZ Company approximately 89 days after they were invoiced. To shorten this management could offer additional incentives for customers to pay earlier such as discounts for prompt payment.

Inventory Turnover

2015: ($150,000 Cost of Goods Sold) / ($45,000 Average Finished Goods) = 3.33
2014: ($160,000 Cost of Goods Sold) / ($20,000 Average Finished Goods) = 8.00

Similar to the above receivable turnover, the inventory turnover tells us XYZ rotated their inventory 3.33 times in 2015.

Again taking the number of days in and year and dividing it by the inventory turnover rate of 3.33, we get 109.61 days. This means XYZ Company stocked finished goods in their inventory on average for 110 days before it is sold. Finished goods inventory on hand needs to be monitored by management because inventory ties up cash via purchases and should be liquidated cash to profit and cash as soon as possible. Management should always balance minimizing inventory on hand with customer demands.

Asset Turnover

2015: ($350,000 Net Sales) / ($474,846 Average Total Assets) = 0.74
2014: ($400,000 Net Sales) / ($220,220 Average Total Assets) = 1.8

XYZ Company turned over assets 0.74 times throughout the 2015 and on average it would have taken 493 for assets to completely turn over.

Profit Margin on Sales

2015: ($45,000 Net Income) / ($350,000 Sales) = 12.9%
2014: ($67,440 Net Income) / ($400,000 Sales) = 16.9%

A 16.9% profit margin effectively means XYZ Company earned $0.17 of profit for every $1.00 of revenue earned in 2014. In 2015 the profit margin fell to 12.9%. Management should investigate the reason for the drop in profit margin which may be a result of a decrease in sales price per unit or an increase in cost of goods sold per unit. This metric is especially useful when comparing companies within a similar industry to determine how efficiently they are producing sales.

Rate of Return on Assets

2015: ($45,000 Net Income) / ($474,846 Average Total Assets) = 9.5%
2014: ($67,440 Net Income) / ($220,220 Average Total Assets) = 30.6%

Similar to profit margin on sales, the return on assets measures the profit derived from each dollar of assets deployed by the entity. The 2014 ratio is misleading because of the $nil opening balance. In 2015 for every $1 of assets invested the company earned $0.095 in net income.

Earnings per Share

($45,000 Net Income) / (100 Common Shares) = $450.00 per share
($67,440 Net Income) / (100 Common Shares) = $674.40 per share

If you owned one share of XYZ Company in 2014 and 2015 your piece of the net income would be $674.40 and $450.00, respectively. This does necessarily mean you would have access to these funds as they are still tied up in the organization. In order for you to receive these funds a dividend is required to be paid or you would have to sell your shares in the company.

Price Earnings Ratio

($100,000 Common Stock Value / 100 Shares) / ($450.00 Earnings per Share) = 2.22
($100 Common Stock Value / 100 Shares) / ($674.40 Earnings per Share) = 0.0015

In the above example we have assumed the market value (price for which a share could be sold to another party) for one share of XYZ Company in 2014 and 2015 was $1 and $100, respectively. A price earnings ratio of 2.22 in 2015 means the cost of earning $1.00 of net income in XYZ Company is $2.22.

Payout Ratio

2015: ($750 Dividends) / ($45,000) = 1.7%
2014: ($900 Dividends) / ($67,440) = 1.3%

Despite a decrease in net income in 2015 XYZ Company increased the portion of net income paid out to shareholders to 1.7%. The dividend per share in 2014 was $9 ($900 dividend / 100 shares) and in 2015 the dividend per share was $7.50 ($750 dividend / 100 shares). In 2015 XYZ Company paid out 1.7% of its total net income in dividends to shareholders' in the year. The remaining net income was kept within the company.

Debt to Total Assets

2015: ($294,000 Total Debt) / ($509,250 Total Assets) = 57.7%

2014: ($303,000 Total Debt) / ($440,441 Total Assets) = 68.8%

In 2014 and 2015 XYZ Company had more assets than external debt. Creditors would take comfort from knowing that even if the company was to be in a default position assets could be liquidated to repay the debt assuming assets could be liquidated for the amounts on the financial statements.

Cash Debt Coverage Ratio

2015: ($190,881 Cash from Operations) / ($385,730 Average Total Liabilities) = 49.5%
2014: ($122,440 Cash from Operations) / ($187,000 Average Total Liabilities) = 65%

XYZ Company generated enough cash from operations in the year to cover 65% and 49.5% of their liabilities in 2014 and 2015, respectively. Given that this is XYZ Company's first year of operations it may be misleading to consider $187,000 the average total liabilities for the period; therefore, 2015 is a better indication of XYZ Company's ability to cover liabilities with cash from operations.

Book Value per Share

2015: ($111,790 Shareholders' Equity) / (100 Outstanding Shares) = $1,117.90
2014: ($66,441 Shareholders' Equity) / (100 Outstanding Shares) = $664.41

If XYZ Company was liquidated at the current statement values and liabilities were paid off at their financial statement amounts each common share would generate a payout $664.41 and $1,117.90 for 2014 and 2015, respectively.

Chapter 6 Summary

- Financial ratios are used by users of the financial statements to further analyze the statements into useful decision making material

- The categories of ratios are liquidity, activity, profitability and coverage

- Using these ratios allow analysts to compare entities within a similar industry in terms risk and benefits

Chapter 7
Managerial Accounting

Recall that financial statements provide internal and external stakeholders financial information and are governed by GAAP. Managerial accounting is the organization of financial data of an entity for internal purposes only that is not governed by any outside regulations.

The purpose of managerial accounting is to provide useful information to management that will enable them to set goals (planning) and to assess whether these goals are being met (control). Whereas external reporting reviews the past performance of an organization, managerial accounting is primarily concerned with future results.

Planning

Planning is a function done by management to determine budget targets and how to best hit them. Organizations typically generate financial budgets to quantify goals and the resources required to achieve these goals. The detail and complexity of a budget depends on the size of the organization. (The budget for a large corporation such as Walmart would have a lot more detail and reports than the budget of your local coffee.)

However, both the Walmart and local coffee shop are similar in that they both have limited access to resources such as money, labour and materials. Therefore, both entities need to budget in such a way to earn maximum rewards when utilizing these resources. The planning function defines financial success for the organization.

Goals and budgets will differ between organizations and industries. Think of a charity that provides collects donations and funds for medical research. The charity is not attempting to maximize bottom line profit within the organization; rather the primary financial goal could be to maximize donations for funding while minimizing administrative costs.

Control

The control function is used by an organization to measure whether the goals set up in the planning function have been met. Organizations often evaluate employees and departments based on the control function. The analyses and results from the control function will feedback into the planning function creating a continuous cycle.

Break-Even Analysis

The break-even analysis is a calculation used to determine the required revenue or unit sales of a product or service to cover costs involved in producing the product or service. It is a useful tool to help management determine the bare minimum of sales required to avoid generating a loss.

Before an organization offers a product or service management should review the costs required to produce the product in order to determine an appropriate price point to sell the product.

The break-even equation is as follows:

SALES PRICE X QUANTITY = FIXED COSTS + (VARIABLE COST X QUANTITY)

Sales Price

Sales price is the dollar amount per unit charged for the product or service.

Quantity

Quantity is the number of units sold and produced.

Fixed Costs

Fixed costs are the amounts spent to produce the product or service that are not affected by the units sold or produce. An example of a fixed cost would be rent.

Variable Costs

Variable costs are expenditures that are dependent on the quantity of units produced. Direct materials and direct labour are example of variable costs

Contribution Margin

The contribution margin is the sales price less the variable costs. The excess sales amount above the variable is applied against the fixed costs.

The above equation tells us that the break-even point occurs when revenue (price x quantity) is equal to fixed costs plus variable costs. Rearranging the equation also tells us:

QUANTITY = (FIXED COSTS) / (PRICE – VARIABLE COST)

EXAMPLE: XYZ Company is considering starting a product but first wants to determine the break-even point for the product for the year. The company is thinking about selling the product for $300 per unit. In order to produce the product XYZ Company will be require the following:

Factory Rental	$200,000/year
Production Insurance	$5,000/year
Direct Materials	$50/unit
Direct Labour	$20/unit

Fixed Costs	
Factory Rental	$200,000
Production Insurance	$5,000
Total Fixed Costs	$205,000
Variance Costs per Unit	
Direct Materials	$50
Direct Labour	$20
Total Variable Costs per Unit	$70
Contribution Margin ($300 Selling Price - $70 Variable Cost)	$230
Break-Even Quantity ($205,000 / $230)	892

Therefore, XYZ Company would be required to sell 892 units of the new product before they started to earn a profit.

Using the same example, let's suppose XYZ Company felt confident they could only sell 600 units of the product and wanted to know the price they would have to charge in order to break-even. Rearranging the break-even equation to isolate the sales price:

SALES PRICE = (FIXED COST) / (QUANTITY) + VARIABLE COST

Sales price = ($205,000) / ($600) + $70 = $412

Therefore, if XYZ Company only felt they could sell 600 units they should at a minimum charge $412 per unit to ensure they earn a profit.

Cost Accounting

Cost accounting is the process in which an organization determines the costs required to produce a product. In the break-even example above the variable costs of direct labour and direct material are fairly straightforward as the cost is already broken out per unit. However, let's assume XYZ Company purchases $100,000 of bulk direct materials for production purposes. How then do we determine the cost of producing each unit?

Let's also assume XYZ Company produces an additional product in the factory. How would management allocate out the rental of the factory to the two different products?

The main focus of cost accounting is putting an accurate dollar figure on products and services when there are pooled or individual costs input into the product. Determining a true cost for each product is important for management to determine the optimal sales mix and price.

There are two main methods of cost accounting that are used depending on the type of product or service being offered. These two methods are known as Job Costing and Process Costing

Job Costing

Job costing is typically used by an organization when each product is unique and different than the next. Think of a construction company that builds houses where each home is different than the next and requires its own materials and labour. Job costing would directly track all the inputs of a specific job or project.

Using this method allows management to budget for each job and track actual expenditures. This is helpful in setting an appropriate selling price during the budgeting stage and when calculating profit or loss at the end of the project.

EXAMPLE: ABC Company builds custom high-end houses for customers. The company requires a 30% margin on each house completed and uses the job costing method to allocate expenses. There are two projects ABC Company is currently reviewing with the following budgeted costs:

Job #1 Budget:

Direct materials $50,000
Direct labour $30,000
Construction overhead $20,000

Job #2 Budget:

Direct materials $100,000
Direct labour $60,000
Construction overhead $40,000

The total expected cost of producing Job #1 is $100,000, therefore ABC Company should charge approximately $143,000 to ensure a 30% sales margin on the job. Sales margin is calculated as follows:

Total Budgeted Cost	$100,000
Sales Margin Required	30%
Selling Price [$100,000 / (1-30%)]	$142,857

Using the same calculation for Job #2 the selling price required for a 30% contribution margin on Job #2 is approximately $286,000 [$200,000 total cost / (1-30%)].

The costs of actually producing each job come in as follows:
Job #1:

Direct materials $45,000
Direct labour $20,000
Construction overhead $21,000
Total cost $$86,000

Job #2:

Direct materials $120,000
Direct labour $65,000
Construction overhead $52,000
Total cost $237,000

Based on the above expenditures ABC Company has the following results:

	Job #1	Job #2
Revenue	$142,857	$285,714
Cost of Goods Sold	$86,000	$237,000
Contribution Margin	$56,857	$48,714
Contribution Margin %	39.8%	17%

Process Costing

Processing costing is used for products that share resources in the manufacturing stage. This method is used when individual products are similar and the process for each product is the same. For example, an organization that manufactures bottled soft drinks. In order to determine the cost of each unit produced departments pool their expenditures and the total cost is divided by the total units produced to arrive at a cost per unit.

EXAMPLE: XYZ Company produces buckets of paint in a manufacturing plant. There are several production departments involved in the manufacturing process. The following department costs were incurred to produce 1,000 buckets of paint:

Prepping/Setup Department $5,000
Processing Department $3,000
Storage Department $2,000
Quality Control Department $1,000
Shipping Department $2,000
Total Costs $13,000

The cost per each unit of production is $13 ($13,000 total cost / 1,000 units produced). If ABC Company required a 20% contribution margin they should sell each unit for $16.25 ($13 / 80%).

Activity-Based Costing

An additional consideration in both methods of costing products is overhead allocation. In the previous examples overhead amounts were provided, however, what if XYZ Company produced more than one type of paint and wanted to apply overhead to each type?

Activity-based costing is used by organizations to allocate shared resources between products and departments. A cost driver is the factor used to determine the portion of cost each product will receive. When choosing a cost driver the organization must consider if there is an appropriate relationship with the cost.

For example, consider a company that produces types of products out of the same manufacturing plant. Each product requires the machinery be prepped and setup before each batch of production commences. The total cost of running the prepping department for the period is $150,000. Assume both products produce the same number of units in the period; however, Product A requires 200 setups, while Product B only requires 50 setups. Under traditional costing each product would receive $75,000 of prepping overhead given that there were equal units produced. Under activity-based costing the number of setups would be an appropriate cost driver and Product A would receive $120,000 ($150,000 cost x 200/250 setups) and Product B would receive $30,000 ($150,000 cost x 50/250).

EXAMPLE: XYZ Company produces two colors of paint, white and black, in a manufacturing plant. Each batch of paint must be done separately. There are several production departments involved in the manufacturing process. The following costs were incurred to produce 600 buckets of white paint and 400 buckets of black paint in the period:

Black paint direct materials $8,000
White paint direct materials $14,000
Total shared direct labour $40,000
Prepping/Setup Department $20,000
Processing Department $30,000
Storage Department $2,000
Quality Control Department $5,000
Shipping Department $10,000

In order to determine the cost to produce the two different types of paint we need to consider the cost drivers associated with each department overhead.

Department	Cost Driver	White Paint	Black Paint	Total
Shared Labour	Labour Hours	800	400	1,200
Prepping	Machine Setups	10	8	18
Processing	Labour Hours	800	400	1,200
Storage	Units Produced	600	400	1,000
Quality Control	Units Produced	600	400	1,000
Shipping	Loads Delivered	2	4	6

Notice for each activity a cost driver is determined for the purpose of allocating out the cost. Using the above cost drivers we will allocate out each department as follows:

Department	White Paint Cost	Black Paint Cost	Total Cost
Direct Materials	$14,000	$8,000	$22,000
Shared Labour	$26,667	$13,333	$40,000
Prepping	$11,111	$8,889	$20,000
Processing	$20,000	$10,000	$30,000
Storage	$1,200	$800	$2,000
Quality Control	$3,000	$2,000	$5,000
Shipping	$3,333	$6,667	$10,000
Total	$79,311	$49,689	$129,000
Cost per Unit	$132.19	$124,.22	$129

If all the above costs were pooled together into one category and divided by the number of units produced the cost per unit would be $129 ($129,000 cost / 1,000 units). Unit the activity-based costing method we are able to determine a much more accurate cost of producing each bucket of paint. These costs should factor into how management sets production levels and pricing of each paint to ensure maximum profitability

Chapter 7 Summary

- Managerial accounting is the analysis of financial information for the purpose of internal business decision-making

- The two main processes within managerial accounting are planning and control

- Planning is the process of setting goals and determining a course of action to meet the set goals

- Control is the continuous monitoring and review of the status of goals and will dictate future planning

- The break-even analysis is a calculation to determine the quantity and sales price required for a product to cover fixed costs

- Cost accounting is used by organizations to determine an accurate cost of producing products or services

- The job costing method of cost accounting is used on products that have a high degree of differentiation among them

- Process costing is used on products that are similar

- Activity-based accounting uses cost drivers to allocate overheads to different product types

- Management should always attempt to accurately calculate the cost of products in order to produce and price them at an optimal amount

Chapter 8
Other Accounting Topics

Business Entities

Organizations are capable of operating under different legal structures. Each country typically has its own laws which govern the types of structures that can be used when operating a business. There are tax and liability benefits within each structure that can need to be considered before appropriately deciding on one. The standard types of structures are sole proprietors, corporations and partnerships.

Sole Proprietorships

A sole proprietorship is an organization that operates under no established structure. This structure requires no legal costs to set up and is not required to file a separate tax return. Typically these are small independent businesses that are owned and managed by the same individual.

Owners of sole proprietorships have no legal protection from liability claims or default action. For example, if a sole proprietorship business was unable to pay its bank loan the owner of the business would be personally responsible for paying the loan.

Corporations

Most medium-large businesses operate under the structure of a corporation. A corporation is deemed to be a separate legal entity under law that is owned and controlled by shareholders. The shareholders appoint the board of directors who make decisions on behalf of the shareholders.

Corporations are taxed separately and differently than individuals. This can be an advantage if corporate tax rates are lower than personally tax rates in the applicable country which will keep more cash in the organization. Corporations are also legally accountable for their actions which can provide protection for the owner of the corporation.

Public corporations are those that are listed on an open stock exchange. General Electric and McDonald's are examples of large corporations that are traded on US stock exchanges. Shares of these companies are traded daily in large volumes. Public corporations must comply with regulatory agencies that are continuously reviewing the actions of corporations to ensure they act in a proper and ethical manner that is in the best interest of the economy.

The main disadvantage of corporations, especially for small businesses, is the professional costs associated with creating the corporation and complying with additional regulations. Legal fees must be paid to register the corporation and accounting costs will be required to comply with tax regulations.

Partnerships

A partnership occurs when separate parties worked together towards a common goal. These parties may be corporations, individuals or informal groups. In certain countries separate legal entities may be create, similar to corporations, which allow for preferable tax treatment and liability shelter.

Internal Control

Internal control is the process in an entity manages the risk of their business. This includes operational effectiveness and efficiency, external and internal financial reporting and compliance with regulations. The process and complexity of internal controls differs depending on the size of the entity but is always present. The framework of an internal control system includes give components.

Control Environment

The control environment is the general attitude of the entity as a whole towards internal control. Management is responsible for fostering an environment of integrity and positive attitude. Think of the impression you are given when walking into a well-run bank branch where employees are friendly and extremely professional. You are confident that they are honest and handling your money with attentiveness.

Risk Assessment

This is the process in which management identifies the areas that are of the greatest concern for the organization. Doing so allows the organization to set relevant policies and procedures to address these risks and provide assurances to management. For instance, an entity may be concerned with extending credit to specific customers. The risk here is that customers may be unable to pay which would hurt the profitability of the organization.

As time goes on the risks of an organization will change due to internal and external factors. Monitoring and reviewing the internal control process should continuously occur within an organization to ensure new and evolving risks are appropriately controlled.

In order for an organization to have effective internal controls the message must be relayed amongst all employees. Fostering an open channel of communication on internal controls within the entity will ensure employees are aware of their responsibilities.

 The control activities are the processes implemented within an organization used to address identified risks. Under the risk assessment component above we discussed an example where an entity was concerned with extending credit to a customer. In order to minimize the risk the organization may require credit checks on all customers requesting sales on credit. Doing a credit check would enable the entity to determine whether the customer has strong repayment history.

There are two types on control activities:

1) A preventative control is one where the risk is address before it takes place. The above credit check example would be considered a preventative control. Another example of a detective control would be requiring two management signatures on checks. The risk associated with checks is that cash could be disbursed to the wrong parties, which would be a misappropriation of funds. Requiring two managers to sign the check ensures two responsible members of the entity are confirming the payment before it is sent.

2) A detective control is an activity that identifies a risk or undesirable occurrence after the fact. For instance, bank reconciliations identify all ins and outs on a bank statement and allow management to ensure the bank balance is correct. These reconciliations are done on transactions that have already occurred and therefore are considered a detective control.

A preventative control is always preferable to a detective control as the risk is managed before the unfavorable action occurs.

Audits

External Audit

An external audit is conducted by an outside professional public accountant on financial information of an organization. The accountant/auditor is required to do work to validate the statements of the entity and then expresses an opinion on the financial statements. The opinions expressed are as follows:

1) Unqualified: This opinion is expressed when the auditor believes that the financial statements accurately reflect the true economics of the entity and are in accordance with the mentioned accounting framework. An unqualified opinion is also known as a clean audit.

2) Qualified: A qualified opinion is expressed when the auditor has reservations about a specific balance or element in the financial statements and will state this concern in the opinion.

3) Adverse: This opinion is used by auditors when the financial statements do not fairly represent the position of the entity in accordance with the accounting framework.

An external audit is important as it provides an objective opinion on the financial position of an organization by trained professionals. These statements are relied on by potential investors and other stakeholders that have a vested interested in the entity and must have rely information on which to base decisions.

Internal Audit

As part of the control process of an entity may conduct internal audits where procedures and policies are reviewed and evaluated to ensure effectiveness and efficiency within the organization. Most large corporations have internal audit departments which are responsible for continuously monitor internal controls within the organization. An internal audit provides assurance to management that the business is operating as planned.

Chapter 8 Summary

- The main business structures are sole proprietorships, corporations and partnerships each with their own costs and benefits

- Internal control is the process in which an organization identifies and mitigates the various risks of their operations

- External audits are conducted by public accountants on the financial statements of an entity to determine if statements are materially accurate

- An internal audit is the process of reviewing and evaluation the policies and procedures used to mitigate risk within an organization

Conclusion
That's All the Accounting You Need! - Where to Go From Here

Congratulations, you've made it through our crash course!

This book has provided the main principles of accounting as it relates to business. Hopefully by reading the material you have gained insight into the main concepts of financial accounting which you can apply to your future business decisions. Having a basic understanding of accounting will allow you to weigh the opportunities and risks within a business and act accordingly.

For some business owners and investors accounting will always be a topic of confusion and frustration, which is fine so long as the importance of accounting is not dismissed. While having an in-depth knowledge of accounting can be beneficial, it is not a necessity. Outsourcing the accounting function in the absence of understanding can be one of the best decisions a business owner can make, thus turning what was once a weakness into strength.

Regardless of whether you find accounting interesting or unbelievably boring it is my hope that you have taken something of value from this reading to turn into future wealth.

Jon Woychyshyn, CPA
William Wyatt

Chapter 1: The Basics of Effective Communication

In a fast-paced world where information is sent and received with just the click of a mouse, it seems that communication is not only essential to function normally each day. For some people, the need to communicate has become instinctive — we rarely pause and think about the entire communication process and if our communication style is effective.

However, most people are still struggling to grasp the concept of communicating effectively. As such, this entire section will be devoted to basic concepts regarding communication and its importance in our lives.

Why do we communicate?

Humans are essentially social beings, and communication is the essential tool that allows us to connect with others. Through communication, we can:

- wield our own sphere of influence among other people, friends and family

- encourage and motivate others into concrete action

- enact changes in our community and social sphere

Types of communication

Communication has a wide spectrum of study, and experts on the field classify it into several subdivisions and types, including the following:

- Verbal communication – this is the most commonly known type of communication; it makes use of words. You use it to communicate with yourself (intrapersonal), with others (interpersonal), and to a large group of people (mass or public).

- Nonverbal communication – also referred to as body language, these are the signals and messages we send and receive without the use of words.

These include gestures, physical appearance, vocal tone, and facial expressions.

- Written communication – a subtype of verbal communication that has to do with written words.

- Oral communication – a subtype of verbal communication where the words are spoken.

- Formal communication – a type of communication which has an official use and purpose, such as lawmaking and communication used and learned in school. Here, you need to follow certain rules and principles in word use and sentence construction.

- Informal communication – casual talk with our family, friends, and colleagues without a distinct set of rules that you need to follow.

In this book, we will be focusing on the use of both verbal and nonverbal communication in casual, social interaction.

The communication process

In order to understand how we can communicate effectively, we need to visualize the process that a message undergoes in order to get across from the sender to the receiver (see fig. 1.1).

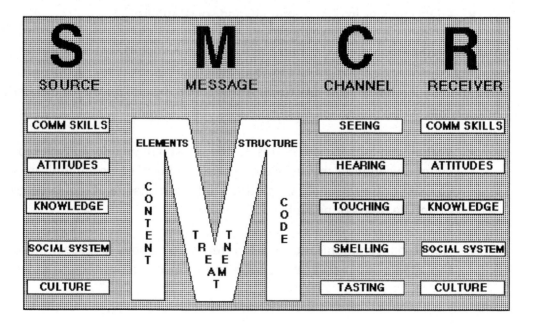

Fig.1.1 SMCR model of communication

In layman's terms, communication is effective if and only if the source or sender has been able to send the message successfully through a certain channel. If it was successful, then the receiver was able to decode the exact same message that was sent, and is able to provide feedback or response to the message.

What hinders effective communication?

Communication barriers are the important deciding factors which can make your attempt to communicate effective or not. If you fail to get your message across, miscommunication ensues, which may lead to other complications such as conflict and tension.

These barriers include:

- Physical barriers, such as doors, walls, and distance between the communicating parties.

- Perceptual barriers or internal barriers such as prejudice against the other party and disinterest in what he or she has to say.

- Emotional barriers, such as fear, anger, or insecurity. These are often sensed by other people and can make it difficult to get your message across.

- Language barriers.

- Cultural barriers.

- Gender barriers.

- Interpersonal barriers, or your instinctive need to hold back in public and avoid opening up to others.

Overcoming barriers

To communicate effectively, you will have to overcome these barriers to get your message across. Overcoming these barriers will require developing and acquiring certain communication skills.

Now that you know the basics of communication and why you can't seem to make other people understand or listen to what you have to say, the rest of the book will discuss tips, tricks, and strategies which can help you improve your communication style. In the next section, we will be discussing the art of listening and why you need this skill.

Chapter 2: Listening – The Forgotten Art to Make Yourself Irreplaceable

The first step to becoming an effective communicator is to become an effective listener. Communication is not just about you or your message! How can you get your message across if you don't even understand what the other party has to say?

According to research, people tend to be bad listeners because we think faster than we talk. That's why it's easier to get lost in thought than to listen attentively to someone else's words.

Why listen?

- *Listening is not the same as hearing.* You might be hearing all the words from the other person, but if your brain refuses to process these words and if certain barriers are in place, you will never be able to understand them. It is a skill that takes time and practice in order to improve.

- *Listening is a sign of empathy and sincerity.* It does not involve simply understanding what is being said. When you listen well, you are able to identify a person's motivations and feelings behind his or her words. It shows that you care about a person's beliefs and opinions and you wish to hear more about them.

- *Listening helps you create lasting connections.* It puts people at ease with you when they feel they can trust their thoughts in you. It helps them open up more, resolving possible internal barriers that have been in place before.

- *Listening relieves tension.* Public speaking can be stressful if you're not used to it, and when your audience isn't listening, it tends to destroy your self-confidence. In contrast, listening indicates a receptive audience, and helps a person relax while speaking.

- *Listening makes communication more efficient.* When you truly listen to a person, you are able to understand the message a lot more clearly, and put a situation in context. It prevents possible miscommunication, misunderstanding, and conflicts among people.

Tips and tricks to improve your listening skills

1. Focus your attention entirely on the person who is speaking. Avoid giving in to distractions, such as taking phone calls or doodling. These activities will likely make you lose interest in the speaker's message.

2. Use all your senses. Don't just listen for the words; you should also take note of the speaker's tone. Look at the speaker intently, studying his or her gestures and facial expressions.

3. Make appropriate responses, but only when the person expects you to. This is why it's crucial to focus your attention — when you miss a cue for response, it might cause the communication process to fail entirely. A simple nod or a "yes" will encourage the speaker to continue and keep the conversation going.

4. Never interrupt the speaker. Not only is it considered rude, it will also cause the speaker to lose concentration on whatever they are saying. Wait for the other party to finish before you share your thoughts, and never attempt to complete their sentences for them.

5. Communication is not a one-way street. It's a give-and-take sharing of ideas. When someone is talking, you should forget about you and your concerns and never attempt to divert the conversation to what you want to talk about.

6. Don't judge. Listen with a clear mind without preconceived notions and prejudice about what the other person has to say. You may not agree with what a person has to say, but listening is about giving them the chance to say it. Prejudice has no place in an effective conversation, and may cause undue conflict between the communicating parties.

7. Engage in the conversation actively. Not because you're on the listening end, you will cease to contribute anything on the conversation. Aside from response cues, you can also confirm what you understood

To check out the rest of "Communication Skills: The Ultimate Guide to Improve Your Communication Skills and Get Your Ideas Across", **click here or go to Amazon and look for it right now!**

Ps: You'll find many more books like these under my name, William Wyatt. Don't miss them! Here's a short list:

- Emotional Intelligence
- Communication Skills
- Persuasion Power
- 7 Reason Why You SUCK at Sales (And What to do About It)

- Introverts Will Rule the World
- Self Discipline NOW

- Charisma NOW
- Much, much more!

About the Author

William Wyatt is a serial entrepreneur, having founded several companies

 throughout his life. He focuses his energies on the achievement of individual success, as he believes every man and women on earth were born to be successful.

He has lead numerous teams within his business career, maximizing each and every time the effects of proper management. During the past two decades he has acquired a powerful set of leadership tools, which in turn allowed him to take his communication & social skills to the next level.

Being a big believer of the importance of self development in every area of life, he's constantly expanding his knowledge and testing out new things. He enjoys sharing experiences with other business leaders as well, as he's certain that surrounding yourself with the right people can indeed skyrocket your life.

Born in 1964, William has a curious mind. He is student of history, always willing to research the lives of great individuals. He defines himself as a "student of infinite mentors", finding in all of them valuable knowledge to be incorporated. William enjoys publishing books that can make a real impact in people's lives. If you have any suggestions or would like to have a certain subject covered in a future book, please send an email to williamwyattbooks@gmail.com and we will get back to you.

Thanks for reading!